PARADISE BY THE SEA

Santa Monica Bay

A pictorial history of Santa Monica,

Venice, Marina del Rey, Ocean Park, Pacific Palisades,

Topanga & Malibu

BY FRED E. BASTEN
INTRODUCTION BY CAROLYN SEE

SANTA MONICA BAY

PARADISE BY THE SEA

Santa Monica Bay

A pictorial history of Santa Monica,

Venice, Marina del Rey, Ocean Park, Pacific Palisades,

Topanga & Malibu

BY FRED E. BASTEN

INTRODUCTION BY CAROLYN SEE

HENNESSEY+INGALLS
Santa Monica 2001

Library of Congress Cataloging-in-Publication Data

Basten, Fred E.
   Santa Monica Bay : paradise by the sea : a pictorial history of Santa Monica, Venice,
Marina del Rey, Ocean Park, Pacific Palisades, Topanga & Malibu / by Fred E. Basten ;
introduction by Carolyn See.
     p. cm.
     Includes index.
     ISBN 0-940512-30-0 (hb)
     1. Santa Monica Bay Region (Calif.)—History, Local—Pictorial works.   I. Title.
F868.L8 B368 2000
979.4'93' 222—dc21

                                         00-063371

Introduction

If you've lived in—or even visited—Santa Monica, Venice, the Marina, the Palisades, scratchy Topanga, or suave Malibu, you find out very quickly that people don't believe you when you talk about these places. They look at you with sour suspicion; they plainly think you're exaggerating when you say, "Down on the canals in Venice we'd stay up all night and party and take coffee out at dawn and stand on the bridges and watch the sun come up and throw pastry crumbs down to the squadrons of golden fish..."

Or, hailing from Topanga, "The raccoons loved our Christmas trees! They'd come out every season, five or six of them, and thump their faces against the glass, trying to get the presents or the lights..." Or, telling them another kind of tale, "Our house disappeared in sheets of smoke and flame. We thought it was gone, our next door neighbor's house went up, but ours was saved, an island in a moonscape of ash."

Or, the Santa Monica Pier! Who wants to hear about the beautiful carousel, and the restaurants—where, again, you'd greet the dawn and not know which way to direct your gaze: out to the great twinkling blue bedspread of the Pacific, or back to the land, where the cliffs of the Palisades look like a bitten cookie, golden, crunchy, good enough to eat.

If people come from "regular" places, even if those places are no farther east than downtown L.A., they won't comprehend the combination of financial and geographical wealth that makes up Malibu—that TV star who lined his house with flags and strode the beaches like a pirate king—and it's a good thing, maybe, the inlanders don't understand, or there'd be a revolution of irate citizens storming the beaches, the canals, the canyons; they live on perfectly good earth, but we got lucky, and we live in Paradise.

Just to prove my point, someone invented Pacific Palisades, where you can have Paradise, and lawns and houses and a hardware store too. See? It can be done. Earth becomes Heaven. Our dreams become reality.

Sometimes those dreams are goofy, even tawdry. Some of these Ocean Park pictures make you wonder about what it is that humans really want. But others—take a look at page 75—prove that not only is this a "gold coast," but we can recognize it! We live here; we live in Paradise.

So, yes, I've had coffee at dawn on the canals and ridden the carousel on the pier more times than I can count, and tapped at my Topanga window and watched a row of raccoons grin in the light of the Christmas tree, and watched my house disappear in smoke and flame. I try to tell people about where I live, but they tend to think I'm exaggerating. No place can be that enchanting, that magical, that filled with whimsy and pleasure and surprise. No place!

Really? Turn these pages. Check out the scenes. Plenty of these places have gone. They've been burnt up, they've slid down cliffs, they've just mouldered and melted away. But plenty of others remain. This is one Paradise you can't pave into a parking lot, because it's too damn various and wonderful. Turn these pages, and take heart. There is a Paradise and people live in it. If you're lucky, you live in it too.

—*Carolyn See*

To Santa Monica Bay
...with love

How It All Began...

Although actual development of the Bay Area did not noticeably begin until the founding of Santa Monica in the mid-1870s, the struggle for possession of this valuable coastline land started taking place much earlier, when the title to the Bay—and all of California—became vested in the King of Spain with the Spanish occupation in 1769. The occupation was begun by Gaspar de Portola at San Diego and was followed by the establishment in California of presidios, missions and pueblos. In 1822, California became Mexican territory. Santa Monica, at this time, was still unoccupied and unclaimed mesa covered with wild grass. There were visitors, however, to the Malibu Rancho, lying northwest of Topanga Canyon, which had been granted in 1804 to Jose Bartolome Tapia. Smugglers, too, had discovered the isolated coves and canyons along the coastline.

In 1827, Xavier Alvarado and Antonio Machado were given a provisional grant to "a place called Santa Monica," referring to Santa Monica Canyon and the land between it and Topanga Canyon, extending to the hills in the rear. Machado gave up his interest to Alvarado in 1831, and when Alvarado died, his sons remained in possession until 1838, when they abandoned "Santa Monica" to Ysidro Reyes and Francisco Marquez.

The first house in Santa Monica was built by landowner Ysidro Reyes in 1839 near Seventh Street and Adelaide Drive—close to the spot where Seventh Street now dips into the Canyon. Reyes originally had settled on a bluff of the Huntington Palisades, but he moved across the canyon, where his sheep would have better protection from marauding animals. Weathered and crumbling, the adobe building was destroyed in 1906.

By the late 1860s, Santa Monica Canyon was being used as a summer resort by travelers from Los Angeles to escape the heat and dust of the city. The visitors pitched canvas tents, enjoyed the sun and surf, lit scattered bonfires and held Saturday-night dances. Despite the merrymaking on their land, the Reyes and Marquez families were very tolerant. Nor did they seem to mind the limited number of establishments that surfaced to cater to the visitors. In 1870, a saloon opened. A year later, a modest motel. Ads in the Los Angeles papers cried, "A week at the beach will add ten years to your life!" Over the next twenty years the popularity of this hideaway spread, as did its glowing publicity: "After a short drive along Ocean Avenue, the Canyon is reached, with its numerous white tents peeping from the green foliage. The Canyon is so filled with wonders that the mind is thrown into a state of pleasurable surprise and ecstacy [sic] when from all sides scenes of enchantment burst upon the vision. Thick clusters of bushes and trees extending a welcome shelter from the hot sun, cool mountain water streams, beds of moss and ferns, shady nooks and tempting lovers' walks. It is all so beautiful, and as you wend your way homeward an impression is felt that only some hours silence alone can satisfy." Santa Monica Canyon was actually the first community—during the summertime, at least—in the Bay Area.

The year after the 1827 Alvarado–Machado grant to "a place called Santa Monica," Don Francisco Sepulveda, soldier and citizen of that growing inland town, Los Angeles, was given possession of and provisional title to "the place called San Vicente," which included all of the original town of Santa Monica. It faced the ocean, extending from Santa Monica Canyon to what is now Pico Boulevard. Inland, it reached almost to today's Westwood region and took in the mountains that overlook the San Fernando Valley.

The two factions that claimed ownership of the rancho would soon be involved in a lengthy dispute over "Santa Monica." They brought cattle, horses and sheep to their new land and established residences. Sepulveda built an adobe house near San Vicente Springs (now West Los Angeles), while Reyes settled on the bluff of the Huntington Palisades (Pacific Palisades) overlooking the Bay. Later, Reyes moved across the canyon (Santa Monica Canyon) to an area where his sheep would have better protection from the wolves. Francisco Marquez settled farther down in the Canyon.

The grant to Francisco Sepulveda was confirmed by California governor Alvarado in December 1839, and with that action the battle began between the Sepulvedas on the one side, and the Reyes and Marquez families on the other. Both claimed ownership of "Santa Monica." The dispute was settled when the Board of Land Commissioners, created in 1851 to investigate and pass upon land titles in California, ruled that Sepulveda would receive "Rancho San Vicente y Santa Monica" with 30,000 acres; Reyes and Marquez procured "Boca de Santa Monica" with 6,600 acres.

In the late 1860s, Santa Monica Canyon was discovered as a summer camping ground by visitors from Los Angeles. The Reyes and Marquez families were very tolerant of the "intruders." On the mesa itself, site of the unborn town of Santa Monica, a trail crossed the grass-covered prairie to the foot of what is now Colorado Avenue. Colonel R. S. Baker, a cattleman from San Francisco by way of Rhode Island, made a trip to the area in 1872, looked over the flat expanse and decided it would make a good sheep ranch. Baker went to the Sepulveda heirs and paid them $55,000 for their rancho. Later, he bought part of the Reyes–Marquez property adjoining on the northwest, plus a portion of Rancho La Ballona bordering San Vicente on the southeast.

Senator John Percival Jones of Nevada, a Comstock mining millionaire, appeared on the scene in 1874 and bought three-fourths interest in Colonel Baker's ranch for $162,500. Together they planned a railroad, a wharf and a town.

On July 10, 1875, a map of "Santa Monica" was recorded in the office of the county recorder in Los Angeles. The townsite fronted on the ocean and was bounded on the northwest by today's Montana Avenue, on the southeast by today's Colorado Avenue and on the northeast by today's Twenty-sixth Street. The Los Angeles newspapers were divided on their new neighbor. One derisively labeled the town "Jonesville" and began attacking it as a deliberate attempt to build a rival city and destroy Los Angeles. Another rallied to Santa Monica's defense and said that by securing the trade of the Inyo silver mines (owned by Senator Jones) and the resulting harbor activity, it would be Los Angeles's savior. A few days later, a much-advertised first sale of lots was held from an auctioneer's stand located near the foot of what is now Wilshire Boulevard. On hand were over 150 people who arrived by steamer from San Francisco, plus nearly 2,000 others, most of whom traveled by stages, wagons and buggies from Los Angeles. The auctioneer was Thomas Fitch, former California congressman and leading orator on the Pacific coast. Standing before an audience of attentive listeners, Fitch announced, "At one o'clock we will sell at public outcry to the highest bidder, the Pacific Ocean, draped with a western sky of scarlet and gold; we will sell a bay filled with white-winged ships; we will sell a southern horizon, rimmed with a choice collection of purple mountains, carved in castles and turrets and domes; we will sell a frostless, bracing, warm, yet languid air,

ABOUT ONE-THIRD THE SITE OF SANTA MONICA,
INCLUDING BUSINESS LOTS, RESIDENCE LOTS, AND VILLA FARMS,
WILL BE OFFERED AT PUBLIC AUCTION,.........................ON THURSDAY, JULY 15, 1875

Terms of sale will be made known through the public press.　　No lots disposed of at private sale until after the auction

For Maps, Pamphlets, and general information in regard to the proposed city, apply at Santa Monica, or at

The San Francisco Office of the Santa Monica Land Company, 330 Pine St., Room 8.

Handbill pinpointing the location of Santa Monica while touting the business, residential and farmland lots for sale at public auction on July 15, 1875. Accompanying descriptive copy boasted, "That Santa Monica is to be the future city of Southern California will be readily conceded after an examination of its many advantages." Among those listed advantages were a soil of "unexampled" fertility, a site of unsurpassed beauty, a harbor where vessels can find shelter in any storm, and the most delightful climate in the world.

braided in and out with sunshine and odored with the breath of flowers. The purchaser of this job lot of climate and scenery will be presented with a deed of land 50 by 150 feet. The title to the land will be guaranteed by the owner. The title to the ocean and the sunset, the hills and the clouds, the breath of life-giving ozone and the song of the birds is guaranteed by the beneficent God who bestowed them in all their beauty."

Auctioneer Fitch sold the first lot, the northeast corner of Ocean Avenue and Utah (today's Broadway), for $510 to a gentleman who also bought four others, all on Ocean Avenue, for $300 each. Over $40,000 worth of Jones' lots were sold the first day; the next day, $43,000 was added in sales.

Within nine months, Santa Monica had one thousand people, 160 houses and half as many tents. Tracks for the Los Angeles & Independence Railroad, sponsored by Senator Jones, had been laid from the ocean to Los Angeles and a wharf was in operation. That same year saw a school district organized, a church established, the beginnings of a public library, a bathhouse, a hotel and a newspaper.

The boom had started. Santa Monica was on its way. So, too, was Santa Monica Bay.

THE SENATOR
AND HIS LADY

John P. Jones, founder of Santa Monica, was born in England and raised in Ohio, and was equally at home in the mines of Virginia City or addressing a roomful of politicians as senator from Nevada. In Washington, where he was a widower (his first wife died shortly after their marriage), he was described as dynamic, fearless, extremely personable and "the catch of the capital." His limited high school education served to trigger his interests rather than deter them. In time, he became a distinguished orator (it is said he had the faculty of making columns of figures sound as fascinating as a novel), an avid student of men and books, a patron of arts and letters and one of the most respected legislators and statesmen of his time—as well as one of the wealthiest. In spite of his fortune, he reportedly cared little for money. Perhaps that is why he was so generous in his gifts to the city he founded and to his adopted country. Colonel Baker's widow, Arcadia, and Senator Jones (who owned three-quarters share of all holdings) donated the parkland at Lincoln and Wilshire Boulevards, innumerable church sites, various public school grounds, the strip of land bordering Ocean Avenue now known as Palisades Park, and 640 acres to the government for the establishment of a National Military Home (the Veterans Administration property) at Sawtelle (now West L.A.).

Georgina Sullivan Jones, the senator's second wife, was the daughter of the Honorable Eugene L. Sullivan, collector of the Port of San Francisco. Tabloids of the day reported that she presided over their Santa Monica home, Miramar, "in a warm, refined, and gracious manner, adding much to the charm of the stately residence." Three daughters (Alice, Marion and Georgina) were born to this marriage.

Above: Senator John P. Jones and his wife, Georgina Sullivan Jones.

"Shoo Fly" Pier, Santa Monica's first, was a dismal loading point for La Brea tar shipments even in its prime. Eventually, it was partially destroyed by fire and the remaining portions had to be leveled. It was at "Shoo Fly" landing that Senator Jones envisioned Santa Monica as an important world port. Barely visible in this photo are horseback riders in the surf.

Right: Santa Monica's first wharf was completed in April 1875. Built by the Jones and Baker interests, the wharf was located approximately 100 yards south of today's Municipal Pier. Steamers from San Francisco arrived at this spot with passengers for the first land sale. Condemned by the Southern Pacific in 1878, the wharf was in operation only three years.

Above: In 1876, Santa Monica boasted 160 homes—and nearly half as many tents—set up on the beach by squatters who took advantage of the relatively unused beach property.

Santa Monica in 1876, one year after its founding. As "gateway to the Inyo silver mines"—located as it was on the proposed route of Senator Jones's Los Angeles & Independence Railroad—the town had attracted a population of one thousand people. Rows of buildings lined Ocean Avenue, Second Street and Third Street for several blocks north of the tracks, and, for a time, it looked like a typical frontier mining town with false fronts, boardwalks and dirt streets. Cattle and stray horses roamed at will, eating the tender young leaves of newly planted trees—and gun-toting residents found great sport in shooting at the circling seagulls. (The illustration was drawn by an unidentified artist shortly after Santa Monica was founded. Although several key buildings were incorrectly located, historians agree that, on the whole, it is a very accurate representation of the Bay at the time.)

The palisades offered spectacular views of the Bay but created an obstacle for anyone wanting to reach the water. By the 1880s, wooden staircases had become a vital link to the shore. The original "99 steps," shown at right, were located at the foot of today's Broadway.

Below: The first "resort development" on Santa Monica Beach was the Santa Monica Bath House. Built by the Los Angeles & Independence Railroad as a draw to the beach, it featured hot steambaths, a plunge and facilities for saltwater bathing. The bathhouse was reached by a staircase leading from the palisades to the sand. This scene was taken about 1884.

COLLAPSE...AND RECOVERY

The crash in Comstock mining securities in the late 1870s took a heavy toll on Senator Jones's fortune. Although he later recouped, he had to abandon his Los Angeles & Independence Railroad (once called the "biggest little railroad in the United States") to rival magnate Collis P. Huntington, who purchased the line for Southern Pacific. In 1878, the final blow fell: Southern Pacific condemned and partially dismantled the Santa Monica wharf. The collapse of mining securities and the loss of the railroad and wharf left the town without hope. Santa Monica's population dwindled to 350. Land sales fell off abruptly. Prices of unimproved land in the county dropped from a high of one hundred dollars per acre to a new low of thirty dollars. Increasing activity "down the street," however, was soon to create an unexpected upswing. Searching for a more convenient terminal near Los Angeles, the Santa Fe Railroad secured a right-of-way between the bustling inland community and the mouth of Ballona Creek, just four miles south of Santa Monica. The town of La Ballona was laid out on paper and an improvement company began dredging a harbor big enough to "float the fleets of the world." By the spring of 1887, two wharves had been built into the surf and a channel was being dug between the ocean and the large inland lagoon. From its connection in Los Angeles, the Santa Fe began laying track toward the coast. Along the way, several towns, including Palms, were born. In August of 1887, the first train reached La Ballona.

Santa Monica Beach, ca. **1898. By the mid-1880s, the tents that dotted the sand had given way to makeshift shanties. This brief period was known as "the beach shack era." The steepled building beyond the pier is the Arcadia Hotel.**

The pier at the Arcadia Hotel.

Whereas the Los Angeles & Independence Railroad had failed to make Santa Monica a transcontinental outlet, the Santa Fe Railroad was accomplishing the job for another town at its very door. Once again, Santa Monica property values began increasing. Jones and Baker were now selling lots near the beach in their Ocean Spray tract (South Santa Monica) and inland as far as Twentieth Street—and prices were climbing rapidly. New business buildings, many of them brick, were rising along Second, Third and Fourth Streets. Elaborate residences, a number in the gingerbread style of the day, appeared on Ocean Avenue and the residential streets surrounding downtown. The boom of 1887 was transforming the face of Santa Monica.

J.W. Scott, the energetic proprietor of the Santa Monica Hotel (the city's first hotel), had reaped enough out of the revival to launch a resort on the south side of town where, on the crown of the palisades, he built the grand Arcadia Hotel.

The Arcadia Hotel, ocean side, ca. 1893.

HOTEL ARCADIA, PACIFIC OCEAN IN THE DISTANCE

Above: Main entrance to the Arcadia Hotel on Ocean Avenue, ca. 1889.
Below: Guests at the Arcadia enjoy a sedate frolic in the surf and could watch the changing sky from the hotel's nearby pier (page 20).

he Arcadia Hotel, on Ocean Avenue between Railroad Avenue (now Colorado) and Front (now Pico), was for many years one of the most distinguished hotels on the Pacific coast, and a true Santa Monica landmark, being the city's first skyline building. Opened in late 1887, it was named for Arcadia Bandini de Baker, wife of Colonel R. S. Baker, co-founder of Santa Monica. Tabloids praised the Arcadia more than any other local hostelry of the period. In 1893, one reported, "The Arcadia Hotel is a first-class, high-grade resort, built upon the finest hotel site on the coast. To the many thousands of patrons of the past, this famous resort has afforded seaside pleasures before unknown and today stands without peer for furnishing true, modernized life at the seashore. In the rear of the house, observatory verandahs, replete with shady nooks, afford delicious after-meal lounging places. Here may be admired at one's ease the rolling ocean, while below extending on either side a distance of several miles, is a sandy beach with thousands of pleasure seekers strolling along, and many hundreds more

Arcadia Terrace, a private walkway from Ocean Avenue to the beach promenade, today marks the site of the Arcadia Hotel.

Santa Monica Canyon's first bathhouse, built in the late 1870s, was owned by Pascual Marquez, son of Francisco Marquez. It was located on the beach against the side of the palisade, just north of the incline where Chautauqua Boulevard is today. The horse-drawn wagon was the Santa Monica Canyon stage, started by a Los Angeles liveryman to take Sunday excursionists to the shore. The stage's route is now Washington Boulevard, the earliest road between Los Angeles and Santa Monica. Ca. 1887.

disporting themselves among the breakers. That this hotel was built for the comfort of the guests is plainly seen by looking over the premises. On the first floor, across from the front entrance, is a well-arranged reception parlor and hotel office in one. On the left is the dining room, which comfortably seats 200 guests and serves more food for one dollar than 18 people can eat. On the right a large hall leads to the sitting room and parlor, also the writing, ladies' billiard, and reading rooms. Directly opposite the main entrance is the elevator which runs to the floors above and two below where the ballroom (site of the social events every season), a conservatory and other places of accommodation are to be found. On the basement floor access to the beach is made, where hot salt-water baths may be enjoyed by those who cannot stand the cold water. The house is furnished throughout with gas and electric light, hot and cold water, bath rooms, and all the modern improvements which conduce to the comfort of guests. In short, we take great pleasure in recommending the Arcadia Hotel to all pleasure seekers and others who visit Santa Monica."

The Spanish graveyard in Santa Monica Canyon was established before 1890 as the burial grounds for the Marquez family by Pascual Marquez. Of the thirty to forty people buried in the small cemetery, Pascual, who died in 1916, was the last. As inscribed on his marker, "Pascual was born here where he is now at rest."

**Mr. and Mrs.
Frederick Hastings
Rindge.**

THE MAN FROM MASSACHUSETTS

I n 1887, Frederick Hastings Rindge, member of a wealthy Massachusetts family, brought his bride, Rhoda May Knight, to live in Los Angeles. That same year he purchased the Malibu Rancho, a Spanish grant. He soon added other lands until his holdings covered twenty-five miles of coast, canyons, mesas and mountain ridges. Four years later, the Rindges moved to their newly completed family home on Ocean Avenue in Santa Monica.

Frederick Rindge was of Puritan stock, and when he came to California he carried with him the beliefs of Evangelism. His influence on the moral and religious history of Santa Monica was strong. He built the town's Methodist Church and was a founder of the Santa Monica branch YMCA that made its home in Ocean Park. His genius and leadership extended beyond local boundaries as well. Rindge helped to found Union Oil Company, Southern California Edison Company and the life insurance firm that became Pacific Mutual. He was also president of the Harvard Club of Los Angeles from its inception until his death, at age forty-eight, in 1905.

The Rindge family home
on Ocean Avenue in Santa
Monica, ca. 1895.

The Rindge ranch
house in Malibu. It
was destroyed by fire
in 1903.

Artist's rendering of Port Ballona, proposed town and harbor on the salt marshes and lagoons midway between Santa Monica and Playa del Rey, 1887. The two piers were under construction when the project was discontinued for lack of funds. The concept was seventy years ahead of its time. Today, the area is the site of the Marina del Rey harbor and channel.

A festive bandwagon, led by a team of horses, draws attention to an 1887 Santa Monica land auction. Prospective buyers were offered five-cent round-trip rides to the auction site.

"PORT OF LOS ANGELES"

As early as January 1888, there were signs that the "Great Boom of '87" was weakening. News from La Ballona was that the Santa Fe might drop the harbor project, finding it "impractical." Not much later, the dredging was halted and the paper town of Ballona was left unbuilt. Throughout the area, land values plummeted and mammoth hotels under construction were abandoned. Even many of the established hotels and resorts were forced to close for lack of business, the elegant Arcadia among them.

It was left to Collis P. Huntington to create the next boom by announcing plans to build a giant wharf just north of Santa Monica, regaining for the town the shipping and trade that had been lost earlier.

In 1891, construction was begun on a new wharf by Huntington for Southern Pacific at the mouth of Potrero Canyon. He named the site "Port of Los Angeles" but residents knew it as "The Long Wharf." Snaking 4,700 feet into the ocean, it was the largest and longest wharf in the world, incorporating two sets of railroad tracks (one standard width, the other narrow gauge) that branched into seven tracks at the 130-foot-wide seaward end. There, a series of coal bunkers, a warehouse with a storage capacity for 8,200 tons, a depot and unloading facilities were located. The docking area could accommodate three coal ships at once and more could be worked if necessary. The Pacific Coast Steamship Company also made "Port of Los Angeles" a regular stop, running steamers from San Francisco. For the traveler, a baggage room and restaurant had been constructed. There was also a special area set aside for sailors and fishermen, with a stairway leading down to a platform and boathouse near the water level.

The Long Wharf had rekindled the old dream of creating a major seaport in Santa Monica Bay, along with creating a new surge of activity within Santa Monica. Business was booming. Hotels and resorts were thriving. And the Arcadia reopened with great fanfare. But the local citizens were not alone in wanting the world's shipping trade and it wasn't long before a "harbor war" erupted between Santa Monica and San Pedro. Santa Monica forces claimed that their city was closer to Los Angeles, the commercial and railroad center of Southern California; that its Bay (by virtue of its shape, depth of water and topography) was more suitable for a deep-sea harbor; that materials for construction of a huge breakwater (one measuring nearly two miles long was planned by the Bay just off Santa Monica Canyon) were nearer and, therefore, would be less expensive; and so on. Advocates of San Pedro claimed the reverse was true on all counts. The controversy raged until 1897, when a decision favoring San Pedro was announced. Work on the new harbor began in 1899.

With the loss of shipping trade, the Long Wharf became little more than a tourist attraction. In 1916, it was reduced to half its original size and made into a fishing pier for residents and visitors. The remaining portion was removed entirely in 1921.

The decision favoring San Pedro was a turning point in the destiny of Santa Monica Bay. Disappointed residents were unaware that their coastline would soon be transformed into one of the most popular resort areas in the world.

The Long Wharf from Huntington Palisades, 1894. In the distance, a steamer rides the horizon line off Point Dume.

Above: Looking shoreward from near the end of the Long Wharf, 1893. The two-track portion leading to land was 3,100 feet long and 28 feet wide, flaring out at the docking area for an additional 1,600 feet to a maximum width of 130 feet. The wharf also had provisions for travelers arriving by steamer. When the first steamer docked in May 1893, more than one thousand local citizens rode Southern Pacific cars up the line to welcome the group. While the Santa Monica town band played, residents swarmed aboard ship and decked it with homegrown flowers. On shore, between Potrero Canyon (left) and Santa Monica Canyon (right), is the escarpment of the Huntington Palisades.

Right: "Port of Los Angeles" from the mouth of Potrero Canyon, 1893. A line of empty coal cars waits to be loaded at bunkers on the wharf's end, where coal, shipped from Vancouver Island, was stored for Southern Pacific. Note the turntable for engines at lower right.

Above: Railroad tracks parallel the shore on their way to the Long Wharf, 1894—now the route of Pacific Coast Highway (U.S. 1).

Below: A train passes through a tunnel as it heads north toward the Long Wharf. Today, the underground curve is the route of Pacific Coast Highway as it passes through McClure Tunnel leading to the entrance of the eastbound Santa Monica Freeway.

Above: "In 1893, the Southern Pacific Railroad Company completed its 4,720-foot wharf which served as a deepwater port for the Los Angeles Area. After San Pedro became Los Angeles's official harbor in 1897, shipping activity at Port Los Angeles declined. Ultimately abandoned and dismantled, no trace remains of what had been the longest wooden pier in the world." So reads the plaques set in a boulder at the site of the Long Wharf, between the water's edge and Pacific Coast Highway opposite Potrero Canyon. Designated as a California Historical Landmark on July 13, 1976.

Below: Today, all that remains of the Long Wharf is a portion of its rocky foundation.

Right: Arch Rock, located on the beach just south of Topanga Canyon, was one of the Bay Area's most popular natural wonders. The arch was so wide that at low tide horse-drawn wagons could pass through the opening. Residents were at a loss to explain what happened to Arch Rock, saying that "it just disappeared." However, on March 24, 1906, after a violent storm, newspapers reported that the arch had "fallen to pieces." It is believed that the rock may have been secretly blasted during the night to enable heavy machines to make their way up the coast to Rindge Ranch.

Below: View north from the Arcadia Hotel with the Long Wharf in the distance, ca. 1893. Stairway-connected buildings in the foreground are part of a complex that comprised the Santa Monica Pavilion Restaurant. According to a pamphlet dated 1893: "This famous family resort has, besides the fine dining room which overlooks the beach and ocean, a number of private dining rooms for parties. Three hundred guests may be seated at one time in the Pavilion and, on a recent Fourth of July, over 1,500 people were dined between the hours of noon and 2:00 p.m. No one should fail to visit the Pavilion Restaurant and while partaking of the good things to be found, enjoy the beautiful scenery and inhale the appetizing ozone." (Just beyond the Pavilion, note the curve of the railroad track as it cuts into the break between the palisades.) In 1893, virtually all of Santa Monica was lit by electricity.

Left: Northeast view from the Arcadia Hotel, overlooking the hotel's gardens and railroad station, ca. 1896. The building at center is the depot for incoming trains. Ocean Avenue bridge at left center crossed over tracks where today's bridge tops the McClure Tunnel. The building to the right is the rebuilt Santa Monica Hotel. The original hotel, constructed in 1875 by Senator Jones and Colonel Baker along Ocean Avenue, midway between Broadway and Railroad Avenue (today's Colorado Avenue), burned to the ground on January 15, 1889. The fire was the first of many to ravage early Santa Monica because of the shortage of water and lack of fire-fighting equipment.

Below: Laying sidewalks along Oregon Street (now Santa Monica Boulevard), 1890. Over the next few years, Santa Monica became noted for its well-developed roads. Several of the main streets were curbed and paved whereas others were oiled. (Sprinklings of ocean water had been tried in an attempt to minimize dust, but the salt content caused mud to form and stick to shoes.)

Below: Same street as seen in 1975. The Bay Cities Building, with its famous clock tower, was Santa Monica's first "skyscraper." It opened in 1929.

Miramar, the estate of Senator John P. Jones, founder of Santa Monica, ca. 1895. Construction of Miramar, located on the grounds of the hotel that now bears its name, the Miramar Sheraton, began in 1887 and was completed two years later at a cost of forty thousand dollars. "The home, with its seventeen bedrooms, was enormous," recalled Dorothy Jones Boden, the senator's granddaughter, in 1974. "He wanted to make sure he had ample room for his mother and her relatives from Cleveland. He loved having everyone with him." Today, the only reminder of Miramar is the giant Moreton Bay fig tree, planted in 1889. "Gone are the orchards, the rose arbors, the tennis court, chicken houses, stable and barn," added Mrs. Boden. "Why, we had livestock right on the property. In those days, the corner of Ocean and California was a cow pasture." Miramar, the largest and most elaborate residence to be found in any of the Southland's beach cities at the time, was razed in 1938.

Left: Christmas party at Miramar, 1897. The senator's young nieces and nephews and their guests gather around the tree during a holiday get-together. Family members are (left of tree) Hal Gorman, Gregory Jones, Mrs. Roy Jones and Dorothy Jones.

"THE PEARL OF THE PACIFIC"

Pacific Electric's "Balloon Route," which brought hordes of summer beachgoers to Santa Monica, helped tide the low period that followed San Pedro's victory in the harbor war. It was the beginning of a constant, unrefined ballyhoo campaign that sparked the growth of the coastal cities. Ads blazed with new catchphrases: "Darling Child of Southland Cities"..."Where Summer Spends the Year"..."The Zenith City by the Sunset Sea"..."The Pearl of the Pacific"..."The Gem by the Sea"..."Mountain Guarded"..."Sun Kissed." No argument was overlooked to drive home the area's matchless climate. Papers reported, "The thermometer has very little to do at Santa Monica other than registering daily the same old story" and openly called the city a "terrestrial paradise where life was pleasant, languid and carefree." As a clinching attraction for the lonely, it was noted that "the glistening sands keep no record of the innocent flirtations of those who indulge in this harmless pastime."

The effect of the campaign was remarkable. Inlanders streamed to the beach, and each summer the hotels, cottages and boardinghouses were filled to capacity. Rivalry with Long Beach and Redondo was intense. When a Long Beach paper claimed that six thousand tourists jammed its city's beaches one Fourth of July, a Santa Monica resident responded, "I don't doubt it.... The overflow from our beaches had to go someplace."

By 1900, it was becoming obvious that the promotional selling job was beginning to have a residual effect. Tourists had seen the advantage of living at the beach and discovered that the 35-minute running time of the electric railway permitted them to live on the coast and work in Los Angeles. Those who came for their health found that the climate alone was enough to get them to stay. Here was the opportunity for a long-awaited revival.

Beginning in 1901, real estate values began to climb once more. Leading the new awakening was an ambitious young man in search of an outlet for his talent as an organizer and promoter. His name was Abbot Kinney.

In 1892, Santa Monica had a resident population of only two thousand but tourists more than doubled that figure. "People from Los Angeles are overrunning the beach both summer and winter," one newspaper reported. By the mid-1990s, approximately 12 million people a year flocked to Santa Monica's shoreline.

Above: Ad from 1902 (Morocco Junction is now Beverly Hills).

Left: Opening Day (April 1, 1896) of Pacific Electric's trolley excursions from Los Angeles to the beach attracted a large number of pleasure seekers—but nothing like what was to come. During the summer, the trains ran almost continually. And the crowds were said to be so thick they seemed to pour out of the cars. The electric train opened a new era of growth for the resort cities.

Above and top: North Beach Bath House, on the strand just north of the Santa Monica fishing pier, was for many years without rival as the area's favorite resort facility. Built in 1894, it was said to have "every improvement that tends to a bather's comfort." A special feature, and one taken advantage of by many thousands annually, were the hot saltwater baths. For the "weak and exhausted," this form of bathing was highly recommended by the medical profession as both "refreshing and strengthening." The admission fee of twenty-five cents was evidently reasonable as the baths were constantly occupied. Attendants, on duty at all times, were described as attentive and courteous. A portion of the building also housed Eckert & Hopf's Restaurant, a bowling pavilion and the first Camera Obscura. In 1902, an auditorium was built nearby, making North Beach the outstanding beach center for tourists, holiday crowds and "hometown" parties.

Main plunge at the North Beach Bath House, ca. 1898. The sideline gallery was often filled with visitors watching the swimmers at play.

Above: D. E. Fletcher, one of "faraway" Topanga Canyon's earliest merchants, stands at the doorway to his general store, the Outside Inn, ca. 1900. Aside from offering gas and oil, tobacco products, ice-cold drinks and groceries for motorists, the establishment rented tent houses, complete with running water for light housekeeping.

Right: Pacific Garden, a favorite lunch stop and gathering place, dominated Ocean Avenue between Utah (now Broadway) and Railroad Avenue (Colorado) at the turn of the century. Said an early pamphlet: "To those who wish a quiet place to eat their lunch, and be protected from the mid-day sun, Pacific Garden is recommended. The refreshment hall is large and the adjoining garden contains seats for many hundreds of people. Every visitor will find everything served promptly and with the best of taste." In the park, directly across the street, a bandstand attracted music lovers.

Left: Another view of the coastline from the tower of the Arcadia Hotel, ca. 1895. The North Beach Bath House, with its pedestrian overpass from the palisade, had only recently been completed.

Looking north toward
Santa Monica from the
Ocean Park beachfront,
ca. 1890. A walk made of
wooden planks permitted
strolling along the sand.

Above: Point Dume in Malibu, ca. 1898. It was somewhere near this point on October 8, 1542, that Juan Cabrillo's high-decked Spanish galleon dropped anchor to survey the landscape of the area. His diary recorded, "A good port; and the country is good with many valleys and plains and trees." The land was also inhabited, as Cabrillo discovered from the many columns of smoke rising from Indian camps or signal fires. His men named the coastline the "Bay of Smokes."

Point Dume, which frames Santa Monica Bay on the west, was named by George Vancouver, an English explorer. Commissioned by King George III to explore California's coastline, Vancouver reached the Malibu area in 1782. Traveling farther up the coast, he stopped at Mission San Buena Ventura, where he met Father Francisco Dumetz. Vancouver named Point Dume after Father Dumetz. (The dome on the point was originally rounded, as shown in the above photo. In later years, the dome was "shaved," or flattened, for possible building development.)

The Whitworth Block.

THE CORNER BLOCKS

Class," in the early days, was having a corner business building and naming it *your* "block." Here are two from 1900: the Whitworth Block, at Second and Utah (now Broadway), and the Keller Block, at Third Street and Utah. On the upper floors of the Keller Block was the forty-five-room Jackson Hotel, described in a publication of that era as "tastefully furnished and supplied with everything necessary for the accommodation of guests. Each room is connected with the office by an electric bell for calling guests in the morning, thus doing away with the old system of knocking on doors and awaking those who do not have to arise until late." The Jackson's dining table was a distinctive feature of the hotel—and reportedly was abundantly supplied with everything the markets of the day could afford. Rooms at the Jackson went for two dollars per day, with special rates for families. The Keller Block, minus its fortress-like roof ornamentation, still stands at the Broadway entrance to the Third Street Promenade.

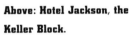

Above: Hotel Jackson, the Keller Block.

Dining room, Hotel Jackson.

Lincoln School on Arizona Avenue, ca. 1902.

FAMOUS CAMERA OBSCURA, SANTA MONICA, CALIF.

CAMERA OBSCURA
FREE TO THE PUBLIC

ADULT RECREATION
CENTER
CHECKERS CHESS
CARDS DOMINOS
FREE TO THE PUBLIC

Camera Obscura, a popular Santa Monica attraction, was newly
housed about 1901 and moved from its location at North
Beach Bath House to Linda Vista Park (renamed
Palisades Park during the 1920s). Then, as today,
Camera Obscura was part of a recreation center that
offered visitors a place to play cards, chess,
checkers and dominoes.

Fashionable houses line Ocean Avenue in this view looking north from Oregon Street (Santa Monica Boulevard), ca. 1900. Even today, sidewalks along this picturesque stretch remain wider than normal to accommodate strollers. (The stand of eucalyptus trees in the park (left) matched those lining the street and were a gift to the city from J. W. Scott, proprietor of the Arcadia Hotel.)

Ocean Avenue today, looking north past Santa Monica Boulevard.

Top: The Hotel Ross may not have had the elegance of the Santa Monica Hotel or the beachfront Arcadia, but it did claim to be "the cheapest and best place in town." Guests enjoyed meals on the premises in the hotel's picturesque dining room and "specialties" in its main-floor grocery store.

Above: View toward Second Street along Arizona Avenue, 1975. The taller building in the distance is the "streamline modern" Shangri-La Hotel. Constructed in 1939 as an apartment building, it was at this time the largest apartment complex to be built in Southern California in ten years. The three-story brick building, built in 1914 as the Hart Apartment Hotel, later became the Mar Vista.

Left: Intersection of Arizona Avenue and Second Street, ca. 1900. Early-day Santa Monicans occasionally referred to themselves as "cottagers." This photo, taken from the upper floor of the Academy of Holy Names on Third Street, shows muddy streets and a group of typical cottages.

SANTA MONICA MERCHANTS 1902

Above: Loring's Lunch Room on Santa Monica's Beach Front Walk opened in 1902 and was a landmark for years. Here, "Bake" Loring (in striped shirt and tie) poses with his family in front of their profitable establishment.

Below: Decades later, after changing hands numerous times, the Lorings' location became popular as Big Dean's "Muscle In" Cafe. Starting in the 1970s, Big Dean's attracted not only beachgoers, bodybuilders, bicyclists, joggers and strollers but such celebrities as Cary Grant, Robert Wagner and Natalie Wood, George C. Scott, Wilt Chamberlain, Evel Knievel and former California governor Jerry Brown.

Top: Saxman & Tegner Grocers, Third Street.

Above: J. C. Crosier, Real Estate, Second Street and Utah (Broadway).

Below: Montgomery's Dry Goods, Third Street.

Top: Santa Monica Steam Laundry, Eighth Street and Railroad (Colorado) Avenue.

Above: M. F. Volkman, Druggist, Third Street.

Top: Sues' Ice Cream & Confectionery, Second Street and Utah (Broadway).

Right: Ad from 1902 for the *Daily Outlook*. The first issue of the *Daily Outlook* (later known as the *Santa Monica Outlook*) was published by Lemuel T. Fisher from his office (above) at the corner of Third Street and Nevada (Wilshire Boulevard) on October 13, 1875, only months after the city was founded. Originally an eight-page weekly, the *Outlook* sold for two dollars per year (subscription price), payable in advance. By the turn of the century, however, the *Outlook* had become a daily and reported news from far beyond the local community.

Bottom: The Pavilion in Santa Monica Canyon was built primarily as a "fun stop" for the many thousands of people who took the popular Southern Pacific excursions to the coast. The huge building was particularly noted for its dance hall and orchestra. Ca. 1902. (The Pavilion had no connection with the Pavilion Restaurant at North Beach in Santa Monica.)

Right: The Pavilion's cavernous dining room could seat over three hundred people.

In 1902, after a long and bitter debate, Santa Monica voters finally agreed to spend $37,161 on the construction of a city hall, to be located at the northwest corner of Fourth Street and Oregon Avenue (Santa Monica Boulevard). The new building was officially occupied in 1903. During this period, telephones were installed in town.

VILLAGE ON THE SANDS

Ocean Park was Abbot Kinney's first real estate development on Santa Monica Bay. Concentrating on providing resort facilities and vacation housing along the beach, he and his partners constructed a small community in less than a decade on land that was formerly sandy waste. In 1901, Ocean Park was a village of two hundred cottages with a post office, stores, a pleasure pier (extending 1,250 feet into the ocean), an auditorium, a racetrack and a casino. The development of Ocean Park coincided with a major influx of newcomers from the midwestern states and, at the same time, a boom in home construction. When the town was incorporated in 1904, there was every indication of rapid growth as both a year-round residential area and a resort. Despite the immediate success of this venture, Kinney was not satisfied. Being a romantic, he began to concentrate on his dream city, the "Venice of America."

The Bath House, Ocean Park, Cal.

Postcard showing the Ocean Park Bath House, ca. 1909. For twenty-five cents, visitors could swim in the huge indoor pool or bathe in saltwater tubs.

THE "BATH BEAUTIFUL"
OCEAN PARK BATH HOUSE
OCEAN PARK, CALIFORNIA

Looking more like an enormous movie set, the Ocean Park Bath House was one of the most talked-about buildings of its day—and a great draw for the beach area. The lavish indoor saltwater plunge (heated for those who didn't take to cooler ocean swimming) was built at a cost of $185,000 by A. R. Fraser, who earlier had been a partner with Abbot Kinney and others in the Ocean Park Improvement Company. The bathhouse is shown here just before completion in 1905.

Fraser's Million Dollar Pier, also known as Ocean Park Pier, taken from the roof of the nearby Ocean Park Bath House, 1911. Angelotti's Hungarian Orchestra was appearing at the huge over-the-water dance hall (below left) while, at the pier's entrance, the Starland Theater featured vaudeville. The pier also offered visitors a scenic railroad, two carousels, a fun house and numerous concessions.

Gateway to the Ocean Park Pier, ca. 1905. This promenade of casinos, cafes and game parlors eventually became Pier Avenue. View looking east.

Tea gardens, cafes, curio shops and even real estate offices helped attract crowds to bustling Pier Avenue, 1905.

Below: Ocean Front Walk, looking south toward Fraser's Pier, ca. 1912.

Ocean Park Casino, 1902. It was considered *the* place for tennis and teas.

Right: Carnation fields in Ocean Park, ca. 1900. A single acre of this experimental garden produced thirty-five thousand carnation blossoms in one season and the carpet of color was one of the advertised tourist attractions on the Santa Fe line from Los Angeles to Ocean Park. The oldest structures still standing in the area are cottages built in the 1890s when these gardens were established—small-frame houses with Victorian ornamentation located on the "Carnation Tract" between Rose and Sunset Avenues, Washington Boulevard and Fourth Street.

View of Ocean Park, ca. 1907.

THE BATTLE FOR MALIBU

Three visitors to Malibu's sprawling Rindge Ranch ride a flat car over the railroad trestle spanning the Ramirez Canyon gorge, early 1900s.

I n 1904, the Southern Pacific Railroad planned to institute condemnation proceedings to get a right-of-way through the privately owned Malibu Rancho, in an attempt to link their tracks, which ended in Santa Monica on the east and in Santa Barbara on the west. The owner of the rancho, Frederick Hastings Rindge, found that he could prevent the railroad from going through his land by building his own 20-mile narrow-gauge railroad along the coastline. It began at Las Flores Canyon and extended up the coast, climbing bluffs and leaping canyons past Point Dume, where it dropped down through a cut in the escarpment. From there, a low bridge carried the rails over the slough (which usually backed up at Zuma Beach) to the shore, following the coastline until it reached the Ventura County line. The railroad was incorporated as the Hueneme, Malibu and Port Los Angeles Railroad. When Rindge died in 1905, he reportedly advised his wife, May, to protect their land from intruders. For seventeen years, starting in 1908, Mrs. Rindge waged a long and bitter battle with county and state officials who were attempting to acquire a right-of-way through the rancho for a coastal road. She erected high fences and hired armed riders to keep out trespassers and surveying parties. Ultimately, she spent a fortune in attorney's fees, carrying four legal actions to the state Supreme Court and two to the United States Supreme Court. In 1925, the Court gave the state of California a right-of-way for a highway, and in 1928 the newly named Roosevelt Highway—now U.S. 1—was completed and opened to traffic.

Above: Cattle graze on the foothills of Ramirez Canyon, ca. 1906.

Right: Ramirez Canyon today—now Paradise Cove—as seen from the pier. The large building (center) is the Sand Castle Restaurant; a mobile-home community is situated atop the hillside. Many scenes for TV shows and motion pictures have been filmed within the private cove, including the long-running (1974–80) television series *The Rockford Files*, which had James Garner's character living in a trailer at the beach.

RENAISSANCE IN VENICE

Actual development in the Venice area began in 1892 when Abbot Kinney, world-traveled connoisseur of art and scenic beauty (and wealthy manufacturer of Sweet Caporal cigarettes), induced the Santa Fe Railroad to extend its tracks northward from Port Ballona, the "dream harbor" that was abandoned in the mid-1880s. Like many other literary men of the time, Kinney was convinced that an American renaissance would rise spontaneously in Los Angeles through the inspiration given by the gentle climate and magnificent natural setting to the vigorous people attracted from the east and midwest. He wanted to design a beach community that would be worthy of such a future—an environment that would foster a cultural awakening. Capitalizing on the similarities between his land and that of Venice, Italy, Kinney actively began in 1900 to build the "Venice of America." He first commissioned architects Norman F. Marsh and C. H. Russell to design the buildings. He then began negotiations with Henry E. Huntington's newly organized Pacific Electric Company to ensure transportation to the site. Huntington constructed the Lagoon Line south from Santa Monica in 1901 and the following year began grading an entirely new route, the Venice Short Line, directly from downtown Los Angeles. Construction of canals, streets and other capital improvements began in late 1904. While in progress, Kinney personally persuaded merchants, hotel men and restaurateurs to build facilities with fronts, at least, in the architectural style of the Venetian Renaissance. All of his exuberance and haste, however, probably led to a number of engineering mistakes, the canal system certainly being the worst. The canals were excavated to a depth of only four feet, the dirt being mounded at the sides by horse-drawn scoop shovels without compaction. Little remedial work was done on the canal floor and the whole project was rushed through during a single winter. The tidal action which, Kinney knew, kept the canals of old Venice wholesome, could not maintain circulation through eight miles of uniformly shallow ditches open to the sea through only one narrow water gate. By 1912, the State Board of Health had served notice that the canals were a menace to public health. No action to close them, however, was taken until Venice's annexation to Los Angeles in 1925. Four years later, the canals of Abbot Kinney's original design were filled and paved as streets, leaving only the grid comprising Carrol, Linnie, Howland and Sherman between Grand and Eastern Canals as waterways.

Abbot Kinney, founder of Venice.

Above: Finishing touches go on the St. Mark Hotel just before its opening, ca. 1905. The hotel, at Windward and Ocean Front Walk, was one of Venice's most distinguished and, in later years, vied with the nearby Waldorf as the place to stay. The Waldorf's guest list included such famous names as Douglas Fairbanks, Rudolph Valentino and Charlie Chaplin.

Left: Looking west across Venice Lagoon (now the traffic circle) toward the Midway Plaisance, an area of amusements, foreign exhibits and freak shows, which opened in 1906. The fanciest of all shoreline developments, Venice was an enormous fantasy. As one old-timer recalled, "Pale imitation it may have been, but the air of constant excitement was genuine...and if the pleasures it afforded were too innocent to match a landscape deliberately suggestive of the sinister delights of the Renaissance, they were nonetheless satisfying. Venice was a collection of gorgeous excesses. Potted palms and pennants lined the streets in constant celebration—of what I was never sure—and the architecture was the grandest, an intricate blend of Italian columns, porticos and balustrades, only slightly marred by the presence of guess-your-weight machines."

V-26. Boating on the Canal, Venice, California.

Above: Postcard showing boats on a Venice canal, 1920s.

Left: The Venice Bath House at the corner of Windward and Coral Canal shortly before opening in 1905. The building contained a heated saltwater plunge and over five hundred dressing rooms. The canals, only recently completed when the photo was taken, had not yet been landscaped.

Boating on the Canal, Venice, California.

Above: Boating along Aldebaran Canal (now Market Street) in Venice, ca. 1909. According to an early Chamber of Commerce report, "At night the canals are lighted by myriads of varicolored electric globes which look like gigantic jewels when reflected in the limpid waters of the street-wide canals." To add romance and authenticity to the scene, Abbot Kinney imported two dozen gondoliers from Venice, Italy, complete with black, silver-prowed gondolas, and repertoires of Italian songs.

Right: Canal scene today.

Windward Avenue, VENICE, Cal.   8537.

Above: Colorful swags decorate an arched colonnade along Windward Avenue in Venice, ca. 1905.

Left: Many of the columns with their ornate capitals may be seen today on a stroll along Windward Avenue.

The Venice Miniature Railway, with its small steam locomotive pulling open-air coaches, ran a two-mile loop on scaled-down track that circled the canal area. Right: Shown at the turnaround point, Windward Avenue and Trolley Way (today's Pacific Avenue), ca. 1909.

Venice Miniature Railway, Windward Avenue, Venice, California.

Above: A view of Venice's Abbot Kinney Pier at night, ca. 1907, showing the Ship Cafe and Auditorium.

Right: Another night scene of Venice's Abbot Kinney Pier, showing the Auditorium, Ship Cafe, and the Dancing Pavilion,

Queen Anne–style house at 1323 Ocean Avenue, built around 1895, is one of Santa Monica's most historic homes. Recently restored, it was once the residence of tennis star Gussie Moran.

A NEW RESPECTABILITY

With Ocean Park and Venice taking up the "carnival spirit," Santa Monica began emphasizing ease of living, the quiet home life and pleasant and cultural surroundings, and finally decided that its true future was in making the most of its natural assets. But while it had unparalleled climate and scenery, it also had a reputation for being a tough town. One irate citizen wrote to the local paper saying, "Passengers on the Balloon Route should be blindfolded while passing through Santa Monica." The town was wide open. Saloons flourished. Park benches and street corners were "strewn with unsavory characters."

The reform was initiated by the influential Frederick Hastings Rindge. He led the fight to close Santa Monica's saloons, offering to personally pay the money the city would lose in license fees...and he won.

By the time the building boom began to subside in 1906 (the Palisades tract—the area between Montana Avenue and Adelaide Drive—was opened just the year before), Santa Monica had thrown off its frontier appearance. No longer did it cater to beach crowds who had abandoned it in favor of Ocean Park and Venice. Once again, the Arcadia Hotel had closed, this time to convert to a private school. As one observer noted, "Santa Monica has no hotel, no first-class restaurant, and offers few attractions for the transient. But it draws a constantly increasing number of permanent residents of the better class." Suddenly, Santa Monica began to rival Pasadena as the "home city" for Southern Californians. Between 1900 and 1905, its population jumped from 3,057 to 7,208.

Residence of N. R. Folsom, Arizona Avenue.

Left to right: Residence of W. T. Gillis, Third Street.

Residence of J. Hauerwaas, Third Street.

Residence of R. R. Tanner, Fourth Street.

Left to right: Residence of J. G. Knesel, Second Street.

Residence of Miss E. Wright, Third Street.

Residence of T. H. Dudley, Fourth Street.

SANTA MONICA

CHURCHES

1902

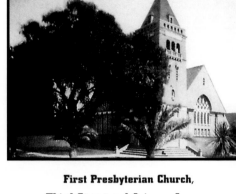

First Church of Christ (Scientist), Oregon Avenue
(Santa Monica Boulevard).

First Presbyterian Church,
Third Street and Arizona Avenue.

Catholic Church, Third Street.

Christian Church, Fifth Street.

Academy of Holy Names, Third Street and
Arizona Avenue.

Methodist Episcopal Church, Fourth Street and
Arizona Avenue.

Left: This combination hose-and-chemical wagon, purchased by the City Council in 1900, was for many years Santa Monica's pride and sole protection. The frame firehouse stood on the south side of Santa Monica Boulevard at Third Street, next to the Santa Monica Bank building. Ca. 1902.

Below: Ocean Park volunteer firefighters in 1902 had only a four-wheel cart to tug to the scene of a fire. The cart was loaded with six hundred feet of hoses, but a limited water supply. The odds of dousing a fire were slim, even if the volunteers arrived in time.

In October 1905, a board was elected to draft a charter for the city of Santa Monica. The following year, the charter was ratified at public election and in 1907 approved by the state legislature. The original townsite had long since overspread its boundaries, particularly on the southeast, where it had gone far beyond Pico Boulevard into La Ballona Rancho.

Andrew Carnegie pledged a gift of $12,500 to build Santa Monica a new library building, provided the city furnish the land as well as a "public free library." A site was found on the northeast corner of Oregon Avenue (Santa Monica Boulevard) and Fifth Street, and on August 11, 1904, the imposing structure was dedicated.

THE INVADERS

anta Monica's reputation as a placid community was shattered in 1908 when an uninvited guest first roared into town: the exuberant young movie industry. Within the next few years, Vitagraph, Kalem and Essanay all had studios in Santa Monica and it wasn't long before residents watched open-mouthed as the young "whippersnappers" began taking over. The moviemakers invaded the beach, backyards and stores to get desired backgrounds, always unannounced. According to one story, one of the town's most respected residents innocently walked out of her front door while a scene (featuring Ben Turpin and "Broncho Billy" Anderson) was being shot on her lawn. She was told in no uncertain terms to get back in the house. "An invasion of madmen," cried a columnist. But the madness ended as abruptly as it had begun. By 1915 the last of the studios had left to join the descent on Hollywood. The only exception was Inceville, founded by Thomas H. Ince in 1913. Fortunately, Ince's studio, home of such heroes and heartthrobs as William S. Hart, Dustin Farnum and Douglas Fairbanks, was too far removed at Santa Ynez Canyon (where Sunset Boulevard meets the sea) to churn the waters down the road.

Opposite: The oldest masonry building in Santa Monica, and possibly the oldest existing building of any kind in the Bay Area, still stands on Second Street between Broadway and Santa Monica Boulevard. It is believed to have been Santa Monica's first City Hall, built in 1873 (the date is interwoven in the grillwork adorning the roof). Some reports say that its days, pre–City Hall, were spent as a saloon, and that "on arrival of the Sunday morning train from Los Angeles, a fresh keg of lager was always tapped for the pleasure seekers." After city officials abandoned it, the building served as a jail, a beer garden (again), a Salvation Army meeting hall and part of the first Vitagraph movie studio. In the early days of the automobile, it also housed a radiator repair shop, a piano tuner and an art gallery. It was designated an official Santa Monica City Landmark in 1975.

Left: Santa Monica Beach and Palisades, ca. 1908. Railroad tracks were removed in 1933.

NATIONAL ACCLAIM

From 1909 through 1919, Santa Monica was the scene of one of the country's premier annual international road races, which attracted such great drivers of the day as Ralph de Palma, Barney Oldfield, Teddy Tetzlaff and Peter de Paolo. The course ran from Ocean Avenue to Wilshire Boulevard, Federal Avenue (in West Los Angeles) to San Vicente Boulevard, and back to Ocean Avenue. Above, drivers prepare for a race as crowds look on from the grandstands on Ocean Avenue near Marguerita Avenue, across from Palisades Park.

Venice, too, had its road races. At right is a souvenir menu presented to "Race Drivers, Friends of the Newspapers and Race Officials" of the 1915 Grand Prix. The luncheon was held at the Ship Cafe on Venice Pier, a short distance from the beachfront road, Speedway, named after the once-annual event.

Far right: A lone automobile chugs along the beach road, north of Santa Monica, on what is now Pacific Coast Highway, ca. 1910.

Venice Road Race

Venice, Cal.
GRAND PRIX
FREE FOR ALL 300 MILES
WED MARCH 17 ST. PATRICK'S DAY

Ship Cafe
Venice, Cal.

Lobster Cocktail

Ripe Olives   Celery en Branche

Coney Island Clam Chowder

Baked Chicken Halibut Colbert
Risolle Potatoes

Combination Fish Salad

Plum Pudding, Hard Sauce

Cheese and Crackers

Cafe Noir

VANGUARD PRESS

ORNAMENTAL
ARCHITECTURE
OF THE PERIOD

Above: Horse-drawn wagons haul supplies to the construction site of the new concrete Santa Monica Municipal Pier in May 1908. Located at the foot of today's Colorado Avenue, it took form between the short stub of the old railroad wharf (left), built by Jones and Baker in 1875, and the longer North Beach fishing pier.

Right: The completed 1,600-foot-long Municipal Pier was dedicated on September 9, 1909, before a crowd of over five thousand spectators. (It wasn't much later that Santa Monica began construction of an esplanade along the beach, a walkway that stretched from Colorado Avenue to Venice.) The new Santa Monica Pier was not trouble free, however. Within a few years, saltwater began to rust the pier's reinforcing steel, causing the concrete pilings to shatter. They were replaced with wood in 1920.

Above: Santa Monica's two piers appear as one, 1916. The smaller Looff Pier, built by Long Beach amusement operator Charles Looff, was the predecessor of today's Newcomb Pier and held the amusement area.

Left: Looff's Hippodrome building (right) opened in 1916 and housed a hand-carved carousel. (The Hippodrome was architecturally designed to be the most prominent structure on the pier, with its domed cupola and octagon-shaped towers.) The Whirlwind Dipper roller coaster replaced the pier's original roller coaster in 1924.

Today's carousel, dating back to 1922, was brought to the pier in 1947 and restored in 1981. It has been seen in many films over the years, among them 1973's *The Sting*, starring Paul Newman and Robert Redford.

Castle Rock, on the beach north of Santa Monica, midway between Beverly (now Sunset) and Topanga Boulevards, was an early tourist attraction. The natural landmark was leveled by dynamite in the 1930s to widen Roosevelt (Pacific Coast) Highway. (Note the man standing atop Castle Rock.)

By legislative act, approved April 10, 1917, the state of California made a grant to the city of Santa Monica in trust for harbor and other public purposes, of the tidelands and submerged lands within the boundaries of the city and below the mean high-tide line. This made the city's waterfront activities possible, including its breakwater (built in 1934) and yacht harbor, for which Santa Monicans voted a $690,000 bond issue in 1931—despite the Great Depression.

Suffragettes led Venice's Fourth of July parade down Windward Avenue in 1916.

Venice canals and shoreline from the air, ca. 1918. Large inland water area (at west end of the Grand Canal) was the Main Lagoon. Triangular area (right center) was "United States Island," a complex of rental bungalows, accessible only by Venetian bridges, where twenty-five families could enjoy resort living in a setting of palm trees and flowers. The massive breakwater at the end of the pier was constructed when the Venice Pier was unable to withstand its first major storm in 1905. To salvage the pier, Abbot Kinney hastily ordered the building of the breakwater (advertised as the only private breakwater in the land) at the seaward end. It proved to be another engineering error, as well as a near financial disaster for Kinney. The breakwater began to divert currents in such a way that the beach severely eroded, and by 1915, waterfront homes were being pounded by high tides. Kinney tried unsuccessfully to reverse the damage for more than 15 years. It wasn't until the construction of the Hyperion Outfall Sewer in the 1930s that the beaches were restored to their natural state.

Beach houses line the road north of Santa Monica Pier, ca. 1916. The pedestrian crossover has changed over the years, but many of the early buildings are still standing.

Right: Villa City, furnished rental cottages along the banks of Venice's Grand Canal, as it appeared in 1918. It was originally known as Tent City (below).

Once completely surrounded by three canals, the bungalows on Altair Place were originally on the site of United States Island. As they appeared in 1978 (right) and today (below).

Picturesque entrance to the Sunset Trail, ca. 1912.

Below: Postcard view of the California Incline, ca. 1915.

Only a portion of the Long Wharf remains in this Bay view from the rustic-railed California Avenue Incline, ca. 1917.

Santa Monica from the air, 1919, showing the early development of the southern portion of the city. The tree-lined street cutting across the upper part of the photo is now Wilshire Boulevard.

Mack Sennett's Bathing Beauties were frequently seen frolicking along the local beaches. This is a behind-the-scenes shot taken during filming of the 1918 comedy *Whose Little Wife Are You?* The Bay Area continues to be a favorite locale for motion picture and television productions.

PARAMOUNT
MACK SENNETT COMEDIES

Above: The Ocean Park firehouse, 1979, vastly upgraded from its turn-of-the-century counterpart. The building has since housed various commercial ventures behind its now-enclosed front and decorative detailing.

Top left: The Ocean Park Library on Main Street is one of the few remaining Carnegie Foundation libraries in Southern California. Built in 1917, the building was designated a Santa Monica City Landmark in 1977.

Venice Short Line conductors stand ready in Santa Monica to transport hundreds of beachgoers back to Los Angeles after the festive July 4, 1916, celebration.

Above: A closer view of Inceville showing a portion of the many sets and village streets used in various film productions. (*Birth of a Nation* was largely made at Inceville.) The studio was destroyed by fire in the early 1920s.

Right: View from Pacific Palisades looking toward Malibu shows Inceville (mid-photo), one of California's early movie studios. Founded by Thomas H. Ince, a pioneering producer (and subject of the William Randolph Hearst yacht scandal in 1924), Inceville was a vast village of movie sets that stretched around the point into Santa Ynez Canyon along what is now Sunset Boulevard. Ca. 1919.

Above: Beachside entrance to Topanga Canyon, 1920. The mesa atop the bordering hillside is today studded with oceanview homes.

Top right: A narrow, winding road, cut out in places from the rugged mountainside, for years made travel through Topanga Canyon a great adventure. Here a car pauses along the dirt roadway to let driver and passengers get a look at the Canyon's first highway bridge, ca. 1920.

Bottom right: Beehive Rock, an early must-see for visitors to Topanga Canyon.

TOPANGA CANYON, CAL.

BEEHIVE ROCK, TOPANGA CANYON, CAL.

Top left: The main entrance to Santa Monica Canyon, ca. 1921. The Golden Butterfly (left center), a bordello in its day, no longer exists, but the building remains.

Bottom left: The pastoral "backcountry" of Santa Monica Canyon, ca. 1923. Building at right center of photo is the old schoolhouse now on the grounds of Canyon Elementary School. The eucalyptus trees lining the Huntington Palisades (right background) were planted by Abbot Kinney as an experiment to discover which species would survive in the coastal climate.

Below: Looking north from near Santa Monica Canyon toward Pacific Palisades and Malibu, ca. 1922. The lighthouse on the point was the landing site for the Long Wharf.

Above and right: The lighthouse at Potrero Canyon, built in 1912, served as Life Guard Headquarters for Will Rogers State Beach in later years. When the structure was demolished in November 1972, the tower was intended for eventual use on the Pepperdine University campus in Malibu but during removal the beacon cupola snapped off and the tower crashed to the ground.

Opposite, top: Santa Monica Canyon, ca. 1920, showing Ocean Avenue leading uphill into Santa Monica. The homes along the flatland overlooking the Canyon are on Adelaide Drive.

Opposite, bottom: Looking north across Santa Monica's easternmost border showing Centinela Avenue (left) looping around on Darlington Avenue, and leading into Carmelina Avenue, ca. 1920. Wilshire Boulevard cuts across lower part of photo. Brentwood Golf Course lies between Montana Avenue and San Vicente Boulevard at top. Bundy Drive winds out of lower right corner.

A GLITTERING TRANSFORMATION

With the dawn of the 1920s, following World War I, the rush of people into Southern California turned into a flood. Los Angeles had two booming industries: oil and motion pictures. Venice and Ocean Park were the "fun capitals" of the coast, if not the world. Santa Monica was being reborn with a new civic spirit, seeing itself as the finest residential community in the United States and the most natural center for "refined pleasures." That image was not to last long, however. In 1921, a group of enthusiastic Angelenos formed the All-Year Club to promote the virtues of the Southland. "California has many glories," the ads modestly cried, "but there is only one Santa Monica." The campaign brought not only waves of tourists but a new breed of residents. Overnight, the town lost its staid, provincial and exclusive character. An extended, full-scale amusement pier, one to rival those down the shore, was born—and the beach-club era was about to begin. In 1922, ornate clubs began to blossom up and down the beach from Ocean Park to Santa Monica Canyon. By 1923, more than fifteen membership organizations were flourishing. The most successful was the Casa Del Mar, which opened in 1924. At its peak, its membership approached nearly two thousand and included such names as composer Rudolf Friml and movie vamp Theda Bara.

**Fourth of July celebration,
Santa Monica Bay, 1920.**

WHERE THE MOUNTAINS
MEET THE SEA
VENICE-OCEAN PARK
SANTA MONICA

Above: This promotional photo was used to attract visitors to the beach area during the early 1920s, a period of extreme migration to Southern California. The setting, climate and economy were all drawing cards, but the glamour and excitement of the fabulous piers received most of the play.

Right: Visitors stroll, sit and lie along picturesque Ocean Park Beach, ca. 1922. Among the attractions on Lick Pier are the Bon Ton Ballroom and Zip roller coaster.

Like a giant glowworm, Santa Monica's famous Whirlwind Dipper roller coaster snaked its way along the brightly lit pier, ca. 1924.

Above: Prestigious Venice Beach, ca. 1920, where celebrities stayed and played. Charlie Chaplin was a frequent guest at the Waldorf Hotel (right). Mae Murray, Janet Gaynor and Norma Shearer had nearby beach houses. Harold Lloyd and William S. Hart had cottages by the canals. Douglas Fairbanks, Rudolph Valentino, Gloria Swanson, Marie Dressler, Mary Pickford and others made frequent trips to Venice, *the* resort town west of the Rockies. Left: Although some of the glamour has faded, the Waldorf is still in operation, now as the Waldorf Apartments.

Far left: The castlelike Deauville Beach Club, located just north of Santa Monica Pier on the site of the old North Beach Bath House, is shown here in 1927, the year it was acquired by the Los Angeles Athletic Club. (After World War II it was sold to a group of film stars that included John Wayne, Joan Crawford and Fred MacMurray.) With its glassed-in private beach, large freshwater plunge and spacious 1,200-seat dining room, the Deauville was considered the most beautiful of all beach clubs. It was torn down in the 1950s after a fire.

Founders' Oaks in
Temescal Canyon, ca.
1900.

"HERE...IS PACIFIC PALISADES"

In the days following the First World War, the Southern California Conference of the Methodist Episcopal Church searched for a place to continue the Pacific Coast Chautauqua Camp meetings. That spot was found on a gently sloping mesa overlooking the Bay. "Here, indeed, is Pacific Palisades," exclaimed Methodist pastor Dr. Merle Smith. In May 1921, the purchase of eleven hundred acres of land was made. For financing, an appeal was made to other Protestant churches, which resulted in the sale of certificates that were later applied to the purchase of lots. On January 14, 1922, the town of Pacific Palisades was founded in a meeting at a site known as Founders' Oaks. The original oaks are gone, but a plaque on Founders' Oaks Island on Haverford Avenue marks the site.

Marker on Founders' Oaks Island commemorates the site where Pacific Palisades was founded in 1922.

Methodist tent village in "Jones Bowl," midway between Temescal Canyon and Beverly (Sunset) Boulevard, was a popular summer playground for the early settlers of Pacific Palisades. The Bowl is now the site of a mobile-home park. Ca. 1922.

Aerial view of Pacific
Palisades, 1923. The street cutting
across the mesa and down the bluff, between
Temescal and Potrero Canyons, is Via de la Paz. The
winding access road to the beach, lit by floodlights at night, was
closed in the late 1920s because of slides.

The "Business Block" at the corner of Antioch and Swarthmore housed
all of the Palisades's early commercial interests. Fear of earthquakes
triggered removal of ornamentation on the roof. Ca. 1923. (The first
structure in Pacific Palisades was the Bishop's Cottage, an unimposing
little wooden house surrounded by miles of barren land, located on the
site of today's Gelson's Market. The cottage originally served as a real
estate sales office and was so named after conversion into a residence
for the local Methodist bishop.)

Left: In 1924, wealthy Adolph Bernheimer purchased seven-plus acres on a mesa overlooking the ocean in Pacific Palisades. For three years, crews worked to transform the former mule camp, a housing site for men and equipment used in the construction of local roadways, into one of the most magnificent gardens in the world. Bernheimer Oriental Gardens attracted an average of five thousand visitors a week to view its elaborate temples, pagodas (one a huge bronze copy of its famous original in China), ancient art objects, waterfalls and ponds set among massive plantings of fuchsias, begonias and lotus blossoms. In 1948, a landslide led to the closing of the property. This photo shows the impressive Sunset Boulevard entrance to the gardens, 1929.

The sprawling Spanish-style building at the overpass on Pacific Coast Highway in Pacific Palisades was built in the 1920s as a community center for the then-new Castellammare development on the hillside above the beach. But it was as Thelma Todd's Sidewalk Cafe—a posh restaurant, gambling casino and hideaway—that it gained worldwide attention. In December 1935, the angel-faced film actress was found dead in her chocolate-colored Phaeton, wearing a twenty-thousand-dollar mink coat and a fortune in jewels, in a garage just up the road. Was it murder—or suicide? The events leading to Thelma Todd's death remain a mystery to this day.

Below and right: Since 1928, the monumental structure rising from the Castellammare hillside overlooking Pacific Coast Highway has intrigued passersby. Often referred to as "the Castle," the thirty-five-room estate, Villa Leon, built by Russian-born Leon Kauffman, has been the source of many rumors, the most widespread (and inaccurate) being that it was the royal home for Prince Aly Kahn and Rita Hayworth after their marriage in 1949.

Left: In 1923, a drive down Wilshire Boulevard in Santa Monica was a quiet drive through the countryside. Left, at what is now the Twenty-third Street intersection (looking east), towering eucalyptus trees line the byway that was destined to become one of the world's most famous and traveled thoroughfares. The following year, 1924, Wilshire was widened. The original plan called for decorative trees, flowers and shrubs, and a succession of historic and artistic arches, obelisks and fountains.

Top: Wilshire at Twenty-third today. The palm trees, flanking the boulevard from Centinela Avenue on the east to Ocean Avenue on the west, were planted during the spring of 1990.

These four panels offer a panoramic view of the Bay Area, ca. 1923. The photos were taken from atop a power pole at the intersection of Fourth and Marine Streets.

Above: Overlooking Ballona marshes (now Marina del Rey), Ocean Park, Venice and Playa del Rey.

Below: Between the Venice and Ocean Park Piers, hotels and apartments line the strand.

**Above: Gateway to the
Ocean Park playground.**

**Below: Across the Bay,
through the haze,
Malibu comes
into view.**

The original Douglas airplane factory on Wilshire Boulevard in Santa Monica, ca. 1921, where the round-the-world planes were built. The location on Wilshire (hidden here by eucalyptus trees), between Twenty-sixth Street and Chelsea, was an abandoned movie studio. It is the site of today's Douglas Park.

The Renowned Clover Field—Start and Finishing Point of the History Making Round The World Flight in the Year 1924

This Field is Now Municipally Owned by the City of Santa Monica. Sketch is of the Municipal Golf Course, Flying Field, Round The World Flight Monument and new Location of the Famous Douglas Airplane Company Factory

Ad from 1924.

I n 1921, an ambitious young man named Donald Douglas, backed by ten men who put up a total of fifteen thousand dollars, began to make airplanes in Santa Monica. Three years later, the first airmen to circle the globe set forth from Clover Field. Four air cruisers carried the name of Santa Monica around the world, and when they returned, 190 days after starting the flight, fifty thousand cheering spectators had gathered to greet them.

Opposite: Spectators gather around the Douglas world cruiser airplanes that successfully completed the six-month, twenty-eight-thousand-mile-long trip. The historic flight began on March 17, 1924. (The scalloped emblems on the sides of the planes pictured a globe with two soaring birds and the words "Air Service USA World Flight.")

South side of the La Monica Ballroom, 1926. In later years, when its glory days as a dance palace had faded, other attractions such as country-western shows lured customers to the renamed Santa Monica Ballroom. Ultimately, the building was transformed into a roller rink. Badly in need of repair, it was demolished in 1962.

Inset: La Monica Ballroom, largest in the world, lit up the nighttime sky from Santa Monica Pier, 1923.

The La Monica Ballroom
on Santa Monica Pier
was billed as the largest
ballroom in the world.
(It could accommodate
ten thousand people
easily—with room to
roam.) Inside, with its
ornamental carvings,
gilt chandeliers, carved
balustrades and
upholstered settees,
the setting was palatial,
reminiscent of some
exotic far-off land, the
vogue in silent movies
of the day. Outside, with
its stylized Byzantine-
domed turrets, the
building looked strangely
fascinating as it "floated"
on pilings above the
surf—a giant arena from
another time and place.

Don Clark and his
La Monica Orchestra,
ca. 1924.

Fire played an important part in the history of the Ocean Park Pier, from the major blazes of 1912 and 1924 to the smaller ones that plagued it during its final days in the early 1970s. Shown here, probably the most disastrous fire of all took place on the morning of Sunday, January 6, 1924. The entire pier was destroyed; losses amounted to over $2 million.

Above: The smoldering remains of the Ocean Park Pier after the fire of 1924.

Right: With the Ocean Park Pier closed, at least temporarily, crowds turned to the Venice Pier and beachfront in even bigger numbers. Here, visitors jam the pier midway, with its towering Dragon Slide and Coal Mine ride (lower right), 1925.

Left: A weekend crowd hugs the Venice Pier for a bathing beauty contest near the Flying Circus ride, 1925.

Below: The Giant Dipper roller coaster on the Venice Pier, 1924. Abbot Kinney continually added improvements and rides to his amusement pier, so there was always something new to discover.

Left and below: The Venice Plunge, built in 1908 on the beachfront just north of the Venice Pier, was a favorite gathering spot. At right is the Venice Amusement Pier with its towering Flying Circus airplane ride.

Bottom: The huge saltwater pool at the Venice Plunge could accommodate two thousand bathers.

After Venice reached its popularity peak in the early 1920s, various celebrations were staged to help promote continued interest in the area. This is Windward Avenue during Mardi Gras, 1925.

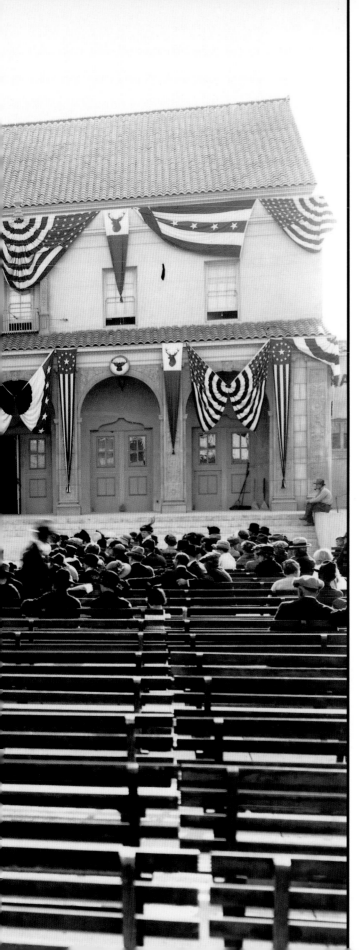

The auditorium in Ocean Park was dedicated on October 21, 1921, and opened with a performance of Gilbert & Sullivan's *The Mikado* by the Los Angeles Opera Company featuring Lawrence Tibbett. The huge hall, with its spacious courtyard and outside seating, was used for community programs until the late 1950s, when it was remodeled for the Westinghouse Enchanted Forest exhibit and administrative offices as part of the Pacific Ocean Park amusement pier. It was destroyed by fire on July 12, 1974.

The Hotel Windermere, a resort on Ocean Avenue midway between Santa Monica Boulevard and Broadway, ca. 1926. The mission-style building was demolished in 1961 to make room for Pacific Plaza, a fifteen-story commercial and residential complex built by architect John Lindsey, husband of actress June Lockhart. (In 1931, the Georgian Hotel would be built just to the north of the Windermere.)

Right: Fleet of municipal buses stands "at the ready" at Hendrick's Corner (southwest corner of Lincoln and Pico Boulevards) to transport riders between Santa Monica and Los Angeles, ca. 1925.

Standing room only, south of the rebuilt Ocean Park Pier at Rose Avenue and Ocean Front Walk, 1926. There were days, old-timers recall, when crowds were so thick it was impossible to get near the beach or the pier, especially on Sundays. The Ocean Park Bath House (right photo), an orphan on the sand in 1905, now seems almost lost within the surrounding spectacle.

In her room on the second floor of the Ocean View Hotel (far right), Aimee Simple McPherson changed into her bathing suit to take her legendary walk into the Pacific on May 18, 1926.

Above: Ad from 1926. With memories of the pier's recent fire still fresh, readers were assured: "All Steel Concrete Construction—Absolutely Fireproof."

Left: The new sixteen-hundred-seat Dome Theatre in Ocean Park featured a lavish interior of Egyptian design, a tie-in with the pier's new Egyptian Ballroom, replacing the theater's previous Spanish decor. Weekend audiences were treated to live vaudeville acts on stage between movies.

Above: The "highway" through Topanga Canyon, 1925. First settled in 1875, the canyon has a rich history dating back as far as five thousand years when primitive Indian tribes roamed the mountains. (Relics have also been found that indicate activity over ten thousand years ago.) Today, residents of Topanga are continually fighting the "battle of the bulldozer" to protect the natural, rustic beauty of their canyon from subdividers.

Left: This totem pole, located in the northerly end—originally called Sunset Point, later Inspiration Point—of Palisades Park, was made for J. Walter Todd in 1925 by the Chilkat Thlinger Indian tribe of Sitka, Alaska. Later that year, Todd presented the giant carving to Santa Monica as a symbol of his love for the city. It has become a landmark.

Below: Pacific Palisades, from Peace Hill to the Bay, 1925. For many years, Peace Hill was marked by a tall white wooden cross, illuminated at night and visible for miles. Eventually, the cross was removed and erected on the tower of Pacific Palisades Community Church. The large building at right center is the Business Block; the canyon at upper right is Temescal.

PACIFIC PALISADES – SEPT. 1925.

Crystal Beach, midway between the Santa Monica and Ocean Park piers, was the site of the popular Crystal Pier, built over the waves at the foot of Hollister Avenue. For a time, however, it was known by a variety of names: the Hollister Pier, the Bristol Pier and the Nat Goodwin Pier, named after the famed Cafe Nat Goodwin, located at the pier's entry.

Above: With the Rendezvous Ballroom as a backdrop, visitors relax on the Crystal Beach sands, late 1920s.

Postcard view of the Bristol Pier, ca. 1910.

Above: Entry to Cafe Nat Goodwin, ca. 1922.

Top right: Cafe Nat Goodwin at night, ca. 1920. Noted a promotional brochure of the period: "A glittering mountain of diamonds could not be more beautiful than Nat Goodwin's cafe when it is festively illuminated." Goodwin, a former actor, called his enterprise "the most beautiful over-the-sea cafe in the world."

Bottom right: The main dining room at Cafe Nat Goodwin, ca. 1918. Other facilities included private banquet halls, a ballroom, a roof garden, a sun parlor and parking for 350 automobiles.

Filming on Crystal Beach, ca. 1927. Santa Monica Pier is in the background.

Below left: This grassy oasis-on-the-beach offered visitors in 1926 a comfortable place to relax and play. The Crystal Beach Pier, seen in the background, was removed in 1949.

Above: The park, with its colonnaded arbor, as it appears today. Located just south of Pico Boulevard, it is one of the oldest parks in the Santa Monica area.

Traffic jam along the
beach between Sunset
and Topanga Canyon
Boulevards in Pacific
Palisades, 1927. (Some
things never change.)

Greta Garbo (left)
relaxes on the beach in
Santa Monica with two
friends from Sweden,
1926. Garbo had only
recently arrived in
Hollywood to appear in
films and was living at
the nearby Miramar
Hotel.

Guarded entrance to the famed Malibu Colony. In 1926, Anna Q. Nilsson of silent-movie fame moved to this private beachfront area and started the celebrity invasion.

The exclusive Malibu Colony beachfront today. Over the years the Colony has been home to such famous residents as Lana Turner, Rod Steiger, Merle Oberon, Gloria Swanson, Paul Newman and Joanne Woodward, Jimmy Stewart and Barbra Streisand.

The Canyon Service station in Santa Monica is believed to be the oldest operating gas station in Los Angeles County. Housed in a small Spanish Colonial revival building, constructed in 1926 by Perfecto Marquez of the original land-grant family, Canyon Service was once the only development in the area and was sustained by the heavy beach traffic. Today it is a favorite of local residents as well, including a number of celebrities who live nearby.

In 1926, Santa Monica's Free Public Library, built in 1904, underwent extensive remodeling and expansion at a cost of fifty thousand dollars. Two wings were added to the original structure and it was architecturally restyled from Greco-Roman to Spanish. The library reopened in 1927. (The interior murals, painted by artist Stanton Macdonald-Wright in 1934, are today in the Smithsonian Institution in Washington, D.C.)

Looking east past the corner of Fourth Street and Santa Monica Boulevard, early 1925. Henshey's Department Store, still under construction, was scheduled to open within the next few months. The building at far left is the Santa Monica City Hall.

Members of the Santa Monica Police Department shotgun squad pose before the cobblestone gates at the Idaho Avenue entrance to Palisades Park, 1927. The Department was established in 1896.

Below: Members of Santa
Monica Bay Telephone
Company's outside
crew gather near the
corner of Colorado and
Cloverfield Avenues in
May 1928. A brick
manufacturing plant
is in the background.

Right: The original
Santa Monica Hospital,
shown here in 1926,
was established a
year earlier by the
Lutheran Hospital of
Southern California.

Left: Looking south down Fourth Street, 1928. The building to the right is the Santa Monica Bay Woman's Club, built in 1914 on land donated by Arcadia Bandini de Baker, wife of Colonel R. S. Baker, the "grandfather" of Santa Monica. Designed by architect Henry C. Hollwedel in Italian Renaissance style, the clubhouse was designated a Santa Monica City Landmark in 1992.

Above: The northwest corner of Fourth Street and Wilshire Boulevard, 1928. The complex is still known as the Wilshire Medical Building, although its exterior appearance was changed during the 1960s from Spanish to contemporary design. (With a thriving population of fifty thousand, Santa Monicans noted, "We are just far enough away from Los Angeles to appreciate her and not close enough to be overwhelmed.")

Above: The intersection of Third Street and Santa Monica Boulevard, late 1920s. For a time it was fashionable for Santa Monicans to tell friends, "Meet you under the clock."

Right: Santa Monica High School, mid-1920s. Built on what was once known as Prospect Hill, the campus has expanded considerably over the years.

Above: Lincoln Junior High School, Santa Monica, 1926. Built in 1898, the building served as the city's high school until 1912, when Santa Monica High School opened.

Left: Clubhouse for Santa Monica Municipal Golf Course at Clover Field, 1928.

Above: Will Rogers, legendary star of rodeos, motion pictures and the Ziegfeld Follies, purchased property in Pacific Palisades in 1922. There, on acreage above Sunset Boulevard, with spectacular views from the city to Santa Monica Bay, he built a small weekend cottage. In 1928, Will, his wife, Betty, and their three children (Will Jr., Mary and Jimmy) moved to the ranch, enlarging the home to its present size of thirty-one rooms.

The Will Rogers Ranch House in Pacific Palisades is the centerpiece of the property, which includes stables, a regulation polo field and hiking trails that lead into the nearby hillsides. The ranch became a state park in 1944 and is today maintained as it was when the family lived there.

The Rogerses' living room at the ranch with its rock fireplace, Indian rugs and baskets. The rope hanging from the ceiling leads to a porch swing that was once lowered into the room.

Horseback riding was a popular diversion in the 1920s, particularly in the Bay Area, where more saddle horses were available than anywhere else in Southern California. (One local stable had more than three hundred of the finest stock in the Southwest.) Enthusiasts had a wide choice of places to ride. There were endless paths along the foothills, quiet trails in the scenic canyons, deserted stretches on the northerly beaches, and even spots within the private estates that bordered the Santa Monica city limits. Active sports enthusiasts were often found participating in matches on polo fields at the Uplifters Ranch and Saddle Club (above) or at Will Rogers's privately owned estate in Pacific Palisades.

A leisurely drive through Santa Monica Canyon in 1927 took sightseers past oak-shaded tents and log cabins. It was from his home on Adelaide Drive, overlooking the Canyon, that famed composer Ferde Grofé wrote his best-known work, *Grand Canyon Suite*, published in 1931. Grofé had originally called his composition *Santa Monica Canyon Suite*, but fearing lack of recognition at the time, he renamed it after the better known Grand Canyon.

SANTA
MONICA
CANYON

Santa Monica Canyon's business district, 1928.

The original Venice Union Polytechnic High School, ca. 1928. In 1922, a young student posed for teacher Howard Weinbreiner, who was sculpting a statue to adorn the main entry to the campus. The girl became famous as actress Myrna Loy, and the statue became a Venice landmark. For over fifty years, it went unharmed except for coats of paint applied by football rivals. In 1979, however, vandals destroyed not only the graceful Loy likeness but the flanking pieces as well, which were restored in 1980. Damaged beyond repair during the Long Beach earthquake of 1933, the original building was later rebuilt as Venice High School.

The Miles Playhouse on Lincoln Boulevard in Lincoln Park was named after J. Euclid Miles, who, in 1925, willed twenty thousand dollars to the city of Santa Monica to build a hall for young people. The Playhouse opened in 1929.

Right: Santa Monica College, formally established as a junior college in 1929, was originally housed in a few upstairs rooms of the high school at Seventh Street and Michigan Avenue. In 1945, the city's adult education program (the old Santa Monica Technical School) and the junior college were merged and, eight years later, these divisions were eliminated, thereby allowing the college to function administratively as a unified institution. Today, Santa Monica College is located on forty-five acres fronting Pico Boulevard between Sixteenth and Twenty-second Streets. The modernistic clock tower is a campus landmark.

Below: Aerial view of the sprawling Santa Monica College campus (center of photo), 1993.

The Central Tower Building on Fourth Street between Santa Monica Boulevard and Broadway. The location was once the home of Santa Monica pioneer Williamson D. Vawter, who developed the city's first transportation system during the 1880s. The building is shown shortly after opening in 1929.

THE GOLD COAST

During the 1920s and 1930s, Santa Monica's beachfront property became famous not only for its high-priced real estate (at the height of the 1920s boom days it reached a peak of twenty thousand dollars per front foot) but for its rich and famous residents and magnificent homes. The area stretched along the coastal strip from approximately Wilshire Boulevard to Santa Monica Canyon and included such well-known homeowners as J. Paul Getty, Louis B. Mayer, Harold Lloyd, Anita Loos, Darryl F. Zanuck, Douglas Fairbanks, Samuel Goldwyn, Mae West, Cary Grant and Marion Davies. The cluster of celebrity homes soon came to be known as Rolls-Royce Row. It is best remembered, however, as the Gold Coast.

Below: Gold Coast homes, ca. 1930.

Above: View of the Gold Coast from Palisades Park, ca. 1940. The large estate (right) belonged to Marion Davies. Built for her by William Randolph Hearst in 1928, it cost $7 million and contained 118 rooms and 55 baths. Many rooms, some dating back to the sixteenth century, were imported from Europe (extracted bodily from palaces and estates) for reassembly on Santa Monica Beach. The property was sold in 1945 for $600,000 and, in 1949, the three-story main house was extensively remodeled and opened to the public as a lavish hotel (Ocean House). Eight years later, it was demolished. The Italian marble swimming pool, cabanas and guest house remain today, used most recently by members of the private Sand and Sea Club, and as a location for the TV series *Beverly Hills 90210*.

Counterclockwise from upper left: Marion Davies poses on the beach in front of her palatial Santa Monica beach house, mid-1930s.

Joel McCrea and his wife, Frances Dee, relax on the sand at their Gold Coast home, 1933.

Aerial view of intersection at Ocean and Montana Avenues (lower left), overlooking the Gold Coast, and the area just south, early 1930s.

The beachfront residence of Irving Thalberg and Norma Shearer, 1931.

The Talmadge sisters, Norma (right) and Constance, at Norma's beach house, ca. 1926.

The Adamson beach house on Vaquero Hill, at the mouth of Malibu Creek and overlooking Surfriders State Beach, was designed by architect Stiles Clement in the early 1920s for Rhoda Adamson, daughter of Frederick and May Rindge. Construction began in 1928 and was completed by 1930. Colorful tiles, designed and made by European craftsmen in Malibu, were used extensively throughout the ten-room house and around the grounds of the thirteen-acre site. Vaquero Hill, one of the last remaining ties to Malibu's historical and cultural heritage, was acquired by the state of California in 1968. The Adamson house and Malibu Lagoon Museum were opened to the public in 1983.

Santa Monica firemen stand attentively with fire trucks to promote a benefit, ca. 1931.

Between classes at Santa Monica High School, ca. 1932.

After winning a gold medal in the four-hundred-meter freestyle swimming competition at the 1932 Summer Olympics in Los Angeles, Buster Crabbe signed a contract with Paramount Pictures and became an honorary Santa Monica lifeguard. Above, Crabbe relaxes for a 1933 publicity photo taken on the Santa Monica Pier.

Left: Beachgoers play along Crystal Beach's sand and surf, just south of Santa Monica Pier, early 1930s.

Above: A racer heads down the narrow Coast Highway (now Pacific Coast Highway) in Pacific Palisades as he nears the finish line of the Olympic cycling race, 1932. Several events of the Summer Olympics, held in Los Angeles from July 30 to August 14, took place in the Santa Monica Bay area.

Right: Spectators cheer a cyclist as he whizzes toward the tape by the pedestrian bridge at Castellammare in Pacific Palisades, 1932.

Above: The polo field at the Riviera Country Club in Pacific Palisades was the venue for Olympic equestrian events during the Summer Games, 1932.

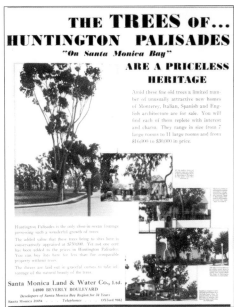

Left: Ad promoting the Huntington Palisades area of Pacific Palisades, 1931.

Below: Pioneer Days Parade, an annual event during the 1930s, drew crowds to Palisades Park to watch the festivities. Here, a horse-drawn float carries the queen and her maids of honor. The celebration also included the municipal band, corps of bagpipes, a whisker-growing contest and parading camels.

Shirley Temple.

The first home of Santa Monica–born child star Shirley Temple is located on Twenty-fourth Street, just south of Montana Avenue. In 1932, the Temple family moved several blocks west to a larger Spanish-style home on Nineteenth Street (below).

Above: Jean Harlow, Hollywood's platinum blonde, and her husband, cinematographer Harold Reason, in the lobby of the Miramar Hotel, 1933. In those days, the entertainment at the Miramar rivaled that of the Hollywood nightspots. Kay Kyser and other big bands played for guests and, for a time, young Betty Grable could be heard—and seen—as a vocalist.

Above: The little one-room schoolhouse on the grounds of Canyon Elementary School in Santa Monica Canyon is said to be the second oldest school building in Los Angeles County. Declared a historical landmark in 1965, it was originally built in 1894 on what is now Sycamore Road. (The Santa Monica Board of Education raised two thousand dollars by taxing the district to acquire a site, building and furnishings, and for payment of salary to a teacher for one year at sixty dollars per month.) In 1933, the school was moved to its location at 421 Entrada Drive, where it served as a student library.

The Galley, Santa Monica's oldest restaurant and bar, opened in 1934. Once a hangout for Errol Flynn and his friends, the atmosphere is heavily nautical with real and created relics, some from the 1935 film classic *Mutiny on the Bounty*.

Top right: Constructing the breakwater off Santa Monica Pier, 1934. The new breakwater created a smooth-water harbor for pleasure boats and broadened the beaches.

Bottom right: Topanga Creek passes under a Roosevelt Highway (now Pacific Coast Highway) bridge on its way into the Bay, mid-1930s. Looking south toward the auto camp and, in the distance, the hillside plateau that is now Sunset Mesa.

Topanga Beach

Left: The Grand Hotel, on the promenade south of Santa Monica Pier, during its heyday in the mid-1930s. Built in 1926 as the Breakers Beach Club, it reopened as the Grand in 1934 with a gala celebration attended by such film stars as Joan Crawford and Jean Harlow. Later, it became known as the Chase Hotel, then the Monica Hotel, and was converted to apartments in the early 1960s as the Sea Castle. Severely damaged in the 1994 Northridge earthquake, the building was razed in 1996.

Below: Detail of underwater mural, south wall of the Sea Castle, 1993.

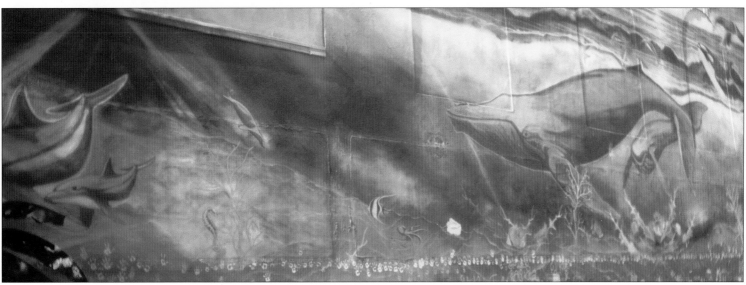

Left: Standing with her back to the Bay, in a heart-shaped mound of flowers at the foot of Wilshire Boulevard, the statue of Saint Monica watches over the city that bears her name. The sculpture is the work of Eugene Morahan and was placed in Palisades Park in 1935. The legend of the city's name dates back to 1769, when Spanish soldiers camped at what is now San Vicente Springs, located on the grounds of University High School in West Los Angeles. With the soldiers was Father Juan Crespi, who called the springs "Santa Monica" because the gentle waters reminded him of the tears Saint Monica wept for her wayward son, who later became Saint Augustine.

Above: The Simonson Motors showroom at Seventeenth Street and Wilshire Boulevard in Santa Monica, shortly after opening in 1937. The building was destroyed by fire in 1986 but was completely rebuilt according to original specifications.

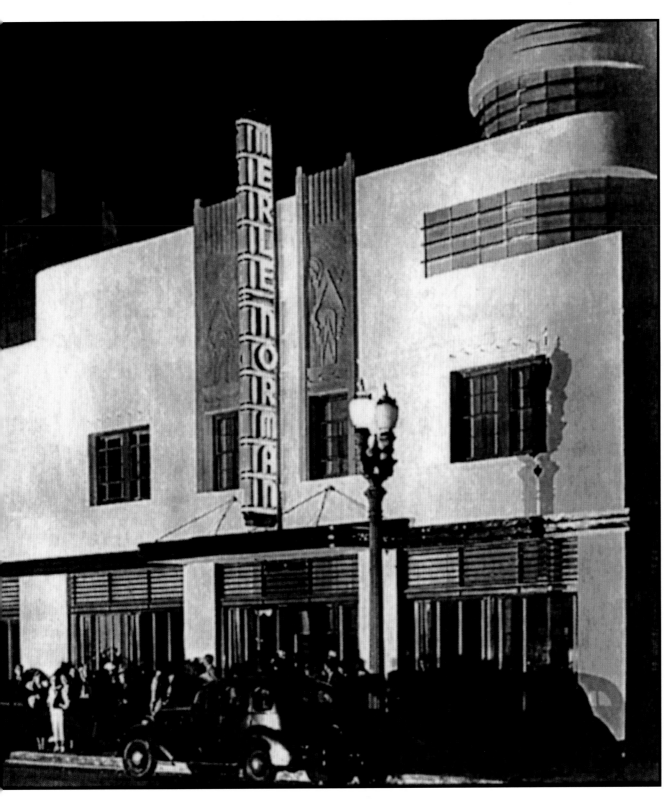

The Art Deco
headquarters for Merle
Norman Cosmetics on
Main Street in Ocean
Park, ca. 1936. Merle
Norman developed her
cosmetics in her Ocean
Park kitchen before
opening her first studio
in 1931. She remained
in the area until 1952,
when the company moved
to Westchester. The
Merle Norman building
still stands at the corner
of Main Street and
Norman Place.

Below: Pacific Electric
trains head south along
Trolley Way (today's
Pacific Avenue), 1940.

Above: Santa Monica's Main Street City Hall began construction in 1938 on property once known as "no-man's-land," acquired from the Southern Pacific Railway Company. The new facility, with its spacious Art Deco—tiled lobby, was built as part of the Depression-era Works Progress Administration to replace the older city hall at Fourth Street and Santa Monica Boulevard. Architect Donald B. Parkinson, along with Joseph P. Estep, helped design such Los Angeles masterpieces as Bullock's Wilshire and Union Station.

Right: The dedication of Santa Monica's new post office took place on July 24, 1938. Here, Santa Monica Postmaster Philip T. ("Pete") Hill presides over the ceremonies that included city officials, dignitaries and their wives. The building was designed in the "moderne" style by architect Robert Dennis Murray. (Postmaster Hill's son, race car driver Phil Hill, is the only American-born Grand Prix Formula One World Champion.)

In March 1938, Southern California was hit with four days of nonstop rainfall, with the heaviest downpour occurring on the last day. This resulted in the biggest Los Angeles flood on record. Losses amounted to over $50 million; 180 lives were lost. Here, in Santa Monica Canyon, floodwaters ran four feet deep, carrying mud and restaurant and household furnishings into the ocean, washing out beach parking lots and structures along the way. Damage to the coastal highway north of Santa Monica was extensive as well, completely clogging roadways and intersections with mud and debris.

Below: Building the overpass from Ocean Avenue to Santa Monica Pier, 1939. It was opened to the public in June 1940.

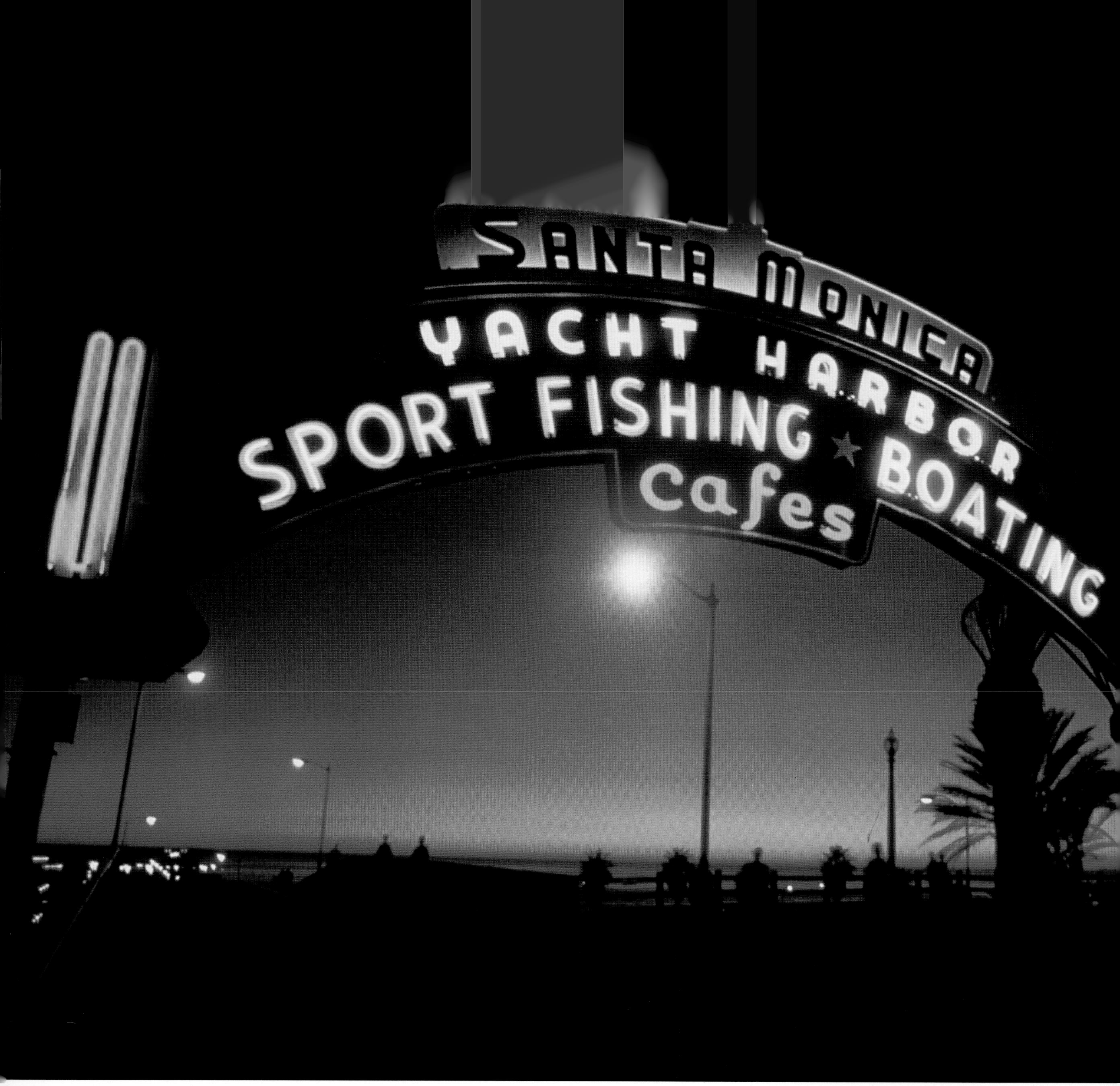
SANTA MONICA
YACHT HARBOR
SPORT FISHING ★ BOATING
Cafes

Far left: With the completion of the new overpass, the Santa Monica Pier Businessmen's Association installed an arched neon sign at the pier's entryway, 1940. The colorful sign has come to be a symbol of Santa Monica.

Top left: Surfing hadn't yet swept the California coast, but it still had a core of enthusiasts, as seen by this gathering taking to the waves south of Santa Monica Pier, 1941.

Bottom left: On Santa Monica's Sorrento Beach, surfers stand with their oversized prewar boards. The man on the right is bodybuilder Vic Tanny.

THE WAR YEARS

anta Monica Bay's contribution to the war effort during the years of World War II (1941-1945) was, in part, the filling of tremendous orders from the government and from foreign countries for aircraft. The Douglas Aircraft Company plant, camouflaged almost to invisibility, expanded its output to break all records. The area swarmed with wartime workers. Barrage balloons, designed to help protect against invasion, together with fighter planes hidden in oddly painted hangars, were decorative additions to the local scene. Blackouts and brownouts were part of the nightly program—and the coastal cities were often packed with servicemen on leave.

Left: Applicants line up for work at Douglas Aircraft plant in Santa Monica. An increase in orders for military planes and a boom in civilian aviation spurred employment.

Right, top: The Douglas Aircraft plant on Ocean Park Boulevard, ca. 1941. At the height of World War II, the huge factory was camouflaged with over 4.5 million feet of net. Fake houses, gardens and trees, with employees tending them, were constructed on the roof to blend in with the surrounding subdivisions. The Douglas operation was used as a model for other war plants and hailed as the finest example of protective obscurement in the world. (Centinela Avenue runs horizontally across photo. [Right center] Clover Field—Santa Monica Airport.)

Right, bottom: Looking east down Ocean Park Boulevard as war workers change shifts at the Douglas plant, 1942. During the peak of wartime production, Douglas was Santa Monica's major employer, with forty-four thousand people on the payroll—half of whom were women.

Searchlights and antiaircraft guns comb the sky for unseen enemy over the Bay Area on February 25, 1942. Photo, snapped during a wartime blackout, clearly shows blobs of light made by exploding shells. Following the nighttime scare, and a report that a Japanese submarine was spotted near Santa Monica, a squadron of blimps from Airship Squadron 32 patrolled the waters off Santa Monica Bay. A harbor foghorn was mounted atop City Hall to warn of impending air raids.

Above: The Sunspot Motel (formerly Carl's Sea & Air Cafe and Motor Apartments) was a favorite nightspot during World War II and for years afterward. Located on Pacific Coast Highway at Potrero Canyon, directly across from the site of the Long Wharf, it featured entertainment, a restaurant and lodgings. Many servicemen came from nearby Santa Monica, where they were living in the hotels and beach clubs that had been taken over by the Army. The Sunspot stayed in business until the early 1980s. Abandoned for years thereafter, the historic, state-of-the-art 1920s building was finally demolished in 1996 after a landslide buried most of it.

Right: The original Saint John's Hospital shortly after opening during the wartime year of 1942. The north wing was added in 1953 (and razed in 1994 after the Northridge earthquake), and the larger south wing opened in 1967. Saint John's is named for John the Apostle and operated by the Sisters of Charity of Leavenworth.

New arrivals to the Bay Area during the war found it almost impossible to obtain housing. Typical living quarters were small, multiunit courtyard bungalows, the apartments of the period, and they could be seen on every street from Ocean Avenue eastward.

Below: A trolley pulls up to the Pacific Electric Station, located in Palisades Park at the foot of Broadway, mid-1940s. Although trolleys were being phased out before World War II to make room for buses, they were back in service during the critical days of wartime gas rationing.

**Postwar scene of the beach
at Santa Monica, 1945.**

SPIRIT...AND GROWTH

The Bay Area moved into the post–World War II era with much the same verve that followed World War I.
It was the 1920s all over again—but without the ballyhoo. New waves of home seekers descended on
the coastal region, more than replacing the Douglas workers who had departed after war production
faded. A furious building boom was launched. New homes, new apartments, new commercial structures
appeared seemingly overnight. With rents frozen and private homes in constant demand, realtors did a raging
business. The mid-1940s marked the beginning of the most incredible period of progress in Santa Monica
Bay's history.

The Malibu Pier, 1949. At the turn of the century, Malibu was virtually an island along the coast, having been cut off from its neighbors by Frederick Rindge's policy of isolation. No through roads existed; trespassers were not welcomed. In 1903, as the sole landing point for supplies for his ranch and railroad, Rindge built the original Malibu Pier, located near the mouth of his Malibu Canyon headquarters. Rebuilt in 1944 after a destructive storm two years earlier, it served as a wartime station for the U.S. Coast Guard. The state of California bought the pier in 1980, but it was again severely damaged in a 1983 storm. Plans to rebuild the pier were announced in 1997.

Malibu Pier

Malibu Beach, California

The Bay Theater on Sunset Boulevard in Pacific Palisades, 1948. Following architect S. Charles Lee's dictum "The show starts on the sidewalk," the much-admired design incorporated eye-catching features. The building was later converted into two separate retail operations: a hardware store and a drugstore.

Above: The Pioneer Days Parade along Ocean Avenue celebrated Santa Monica's seventy-fifth anniversary in 1950. The parade featured bands, horses, wagons, carriages and two thousand square dancers from all parts of the country.

Left: When the Venice Pier closed in 1946, it marked the end of an era in Venice. (The Los Angeles Department of Parks and Recreation, which had taken over the lease in 1946, had other plans for the beach area.) The closure, and demolition in 1947, was a boon to the Ocean Park Pier. Here, looking north from Windward Avenue, is the nearly deserted Ocean Front Walk, 1949. Many of the beachside buildings have disappeared; once-thriving businesses are shuttered. *Slattery's Hurricane* was playing at the Venice Theater.

Trinity Baptist Church on California Avenue as it appeared in its opening year, 1950. The new church replaced an earlier structure.

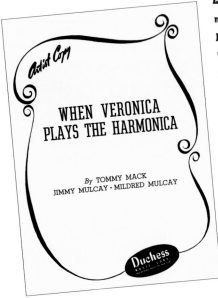

Artist Copy

WHEN VERONICA
PLAYS THE HARMONICA

By TOMMY MACK
JIMMY MULCAY · MILDRED MULCAY

Duchess

Left: Sheet music from the 1948 novelty song made popular by Kay Kyser and his orchestra. The lyric had Veronica playing the harmonica "down on the pier at Santa Monica."

Right: Ocean Avenue entrance to the Miramar Hotel and bungalows, ca. 1950.

Top right: The Self-Realization Fellowship Temple, known as Lake Shrine, in Pacific Palisades was dedicated in 1950 by California lieutenant governor Goodwin J. Knight. The open-air temple, distinguished by its striking golden lotus columns, overlooks a two-acre natural lake.

Below: The Gandhi World Peace Memorial. Nearby is a bo tree, descendant of a twenty-six-hundred-year-old tree in India.

Bottom right: Rippling water near Topanga Creek Shopping Center in Topanga Canyon. During rainy season, runoff from surrounding mountains often turns the creek into a rushing river. Topanga Canyon Boulevard crosses at bridge (top center).

Santa Monica's Gold Coast, 1951. The two-story home with the long, fenced-in oceanside yard (second from bottom) belonged to Mrs. J. Paul Getty. It was replaced in 1995 with a condominium. Note how the beach has widened since the breakwater was installed in 1934.

WILL ROGERS HIGHWAY
DEDICATED 1952
TO
WILL ROGERS
HUMORIST · WORLD TRAVELER · GOOD NEIGHBOR
THIS MAIN STREET OF AMERICA
HIGHWAY 66
WAS THE FIRST ROAD HE TRAVELED IN
A CAREER THAT LED HIM STRAIGHT TO
THE HEARTS OF HIS COUNTRYMEN

US 66

Plaque dedicated to humorist Will Rogers in 1952, naming Highway 66 as the Will Rogers Highway. The marker is located in Palisades Park between walkways opposite the end of "Route 66" (Santa Monica Boulevard), as it was more commonly known.

Since 1954, Santa Monica has been the "City of the Christmas Story." Each December, local churches participate in the design and display of Nativity scenes depicting, in sequence, the life of Christ. Up to a dozen nineteen-foot "mangers" line a two-and-a-half-block stretch in Palisades Park from Wilshire Boulevard south, where visitors may view the scenes either in their cars or on foot. The tradition began with opening ceremonies, held on the first Monday in December, and included a "Singing Cross Parade" to the park, where crowds were serenaded with carols. (With the 1996 Christmas season, Santa Monica began another tradition: the lighting of a towering Christmas tree at the Wilshire Boulevard entrance to the Third Street Promenade.)

Clockwise from top right: On September 12, 1955, Paul Revere Junior High School (now Middle School) admitted its first students. The campus is located on what was once the northernmost polo field of the Riviera Country Club.

The Belle-Vue Restaurant at Ocean Avenue and Santa Monica Boulevard, 1956. The building previously housed La Monica Motors, a dealer for Rickenbacker automobiles.

The famous Malibu Colony from above Malibu Colony Road, ca. 1955.

Looking across Palisades Park toward Malibu from near Washington Avenue, ca. 1955.

Opposite and left: Muscle Beach, July 4, 1956. This world-famous spot, just south of Santa Monica Pier, was noted not only for its exhibitions of strength and agility but for its colorful crowds as well.

The discovery of oil on the Venice peninsula (now the Marina peninsula) in 1929 triggered the start of derrick fever. Although a gradual decline in production began in the 1930s, many of the rigs remained until 1974. Below, view looking south along the canal area in the mid-1950s.

OCEAN PARK PIER

Expansion and remodeling of the Ocean Park Pier in 1957 prior to its reopening as Pacific Ocean Park (POP). Until the new amusement center opened, the pier's carnival atmosphere, complete with fun houses and arcades, was the main attraction.

Above: Ocean Skyway bubble cars travel over the waters of the Bay as they make their way along the length of the POP pier.

Left: Neptune's Courtyard, theme building and entrance to Pacific Ocean Park. The new twenty-eight-acre playground opened on July 28, 1958, attracting more customers than Disneyland during its first week in operation.

Below: Mystery Island, at the tip of the pier, was the park's most imaginative attraction. Visitors crossed a suspension bridge over a waterfall to board the Banana Train ride for a journey that included a simulated earthquake, a tropical rainstorm, spouting geysers, spider caves and an erupting volcano.

dance to
LAWRENCE WELK
Pacific Ocean Park pop
ARAGON BALLROOM
SANTA MONICA

Pacific Ocean Park's midway with its fun houses and thrill rides.

MAGIC CARPET

MAGIC CAR

FUN FOREST

FUN FOREST

Pacific Ocean Park drew large crowds during its early years (1965 was the most successful, attracting over 1.6 million customers), but financial problems and dwindling attendance forced the owners into bankruptcy in 1967. Abandoned, the park's buildings fell into disrepair and prey to several fires. POP was demolished during 1973–74 and the area was cleared to provide an uninterrupted sweep of beach.

Santa Monica Civic Auditorium first opened its doors in 1958. Designed by architect Welton Beckett, the Civic has played host to a wide variety of attractions, from theater-in-the-round and collectible shows to conventions, exhibitions and food fairs. It is probably best remembered, however, as the site of the Academy Awards (from 1961 to 1968) and rock concerts spotlighting such stars as Rod Stewart, Mick Jagger, Elton John, David Bowie, James Brown, the Eagles, Bob Dylan, Santana and many others.

Left: Looking north along Santa Monica's Third Street from near Santa Monica Boulevard, 1957.

Below left: The newest restaurant/bar on Ocean Avenue in 1959 was Chez Jay, run by sportsman/ adventurer Jay Fiondella. It had a Dutch door and sawdust on the floor, and was filled with memorabilia from the proprietor's exploits.

Below right: Interior of the Malibu Sea Lion restaurant, which boasted the world's longest oceanfront dining room, ca. 1959. A live seal was kept in a tank in the parking lot.

Above: Until 1961, the curve at Adelaide Drive and Ocean Avenue had drivers speeding around the bend, often veering into the opposing lane. The installation of a safety "island" helped calm traffic.

Right: Looking toward Pacific Palisades from Ocean and California Avenues, 1959. A portion of the California Incline can be seen at far left. The vacant land in the lower right corner is the future site of the fourteen-story Santa Monica Bay Towers, built in the early 1960s.

For decades, the beaches of Santa Monica Bay had been a favorite gathering spot to celebrate the Fourth of July, drawing millions of visitors annually to spend a day in the sun and then watch the fireworks displays staged by private clubs or partying individuals. In 1961, Santa Monica added its own touch to the nighttime festivities with spectacular pyrotechnics launched from the pier. The attraction created such enormous safety and traffic problems—Pacific Coast Highway and the freeway tunnel became parking lots—that the fireworks were rescheduled to the early morning hours of July 4 in 1988. Ongoing concerns forced cancellation of the annual fireworks displays in 1994.

President John F. Kennedy drew a big crowd as he arrived at the Santa Monica home of Peter Lawford and Patricia Kennedy in June 1963. Both President Kennedy and his brother, Attorney General Robert Kennedy, were visitors to the beach house, the former residence of Louis B. Mayer, while they were in office.

Right: Construction on the central section of Santa Monica's County Building, on the grassy slope adjacent to City Hall, began in 1950. Shortly after, the north wing was added. In 1964, the larger south wing was dedicated.

Above: Looking east on Montana Avenue from Twelfth Street, 1965.

Left, top and bottom: Santa Monica's Main Library opened in new quarters in 1965, one block east of its earlier location at Fifth Street and Santa Monica Boulevard. The Main Library and its three city branches contain over 350,000 books in its adult and juvenile collections plus holdings that include government documents, periodicals, pamphlets, recordings and films.

The Miramar Hotel's new 10-story Tower wing, constructed during 1959–60, as seen in 1964. Scenes for numerous films and TV series were shot at the Miramar during the 1960s, including the swimming pool scene with Doris Day and Cary Grant for *That Touch of Mink,* (1962).

Douglas Aircraft Company, Clover Field, and area surrounding Ocean Park Boulevard, 1955.

The high, curving walls of the Venice Pavilion, on the beach at Windward Avenue, surround an indoor performing theater and outside areas for picnics, sunning and recreational activities. The Pavilion opened in the early 1960s.

Above: View south down Third Street across Broadway, 1963.

Tearing up Third Street for the new pedestrian mall, near Santa Monica Boulevard, 1964.

A NEW LOOK FOR THIRD STREET

By the early 1960s, the opening of shopping centers and malls in outlying areas had drastically curtailed business along downtown Santa Monica's Third Street. In 1964, construction began on a new pedestrian-only Third Street Mall in the hope that a revitalized shopping district would bring customers back. It opened to great fanfare in 1965.

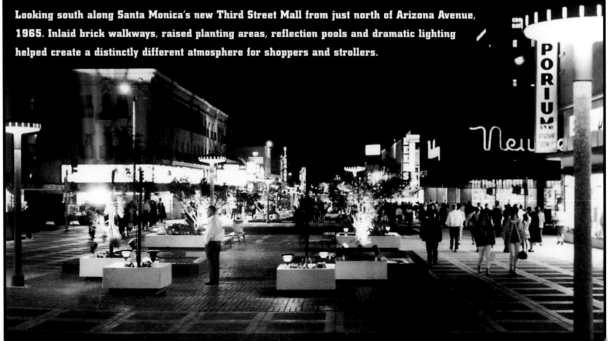

Looking south along Santa Monica's new Third Street Mall from just north of Arizona Avenue, 1965. Inlaid brick walkways, raised planting areas, reflection pools and dramatic lighting helped create a distinctly different atmosphere for shoppers and strollers.

Above: A historic fountain greeted visitors at the Wilshire Boulevard entrance to the new Third Street Mall. The work of sculptor Merrill Gage, it contained six cast-concrete panels that depicted Santa Monica's past from the days of the ranchos to the 1924 round-the-world flight by the Douglas planes.

Below: Picture-postcard view overlooking the area north of California Avenue from a perch high above Second Street, 1965.

Right: Actress Natalie Wood runs along Santa Monica Pier's boardwalk as she rehearses a scene for the 1965 Warner Bros. film *Inside Daisy Clover*. (Angel Beach, seen on the parking sign, is a fictitious name created for the movie.)

MARINA DEL REY

The marshlands of La Ballona had been favored hunting grounds from early Indian days to modern times. The last of the duck blinds were still standing in 1957 when dredging began for Marina del Rey ("Harbor of the King"). The Marina opened in 1962 and was officially dedicated on April 10, 1965. Slow growth and breakwater difficulties plagued its first two years, and then everything began to look just as the early brochures said it would. Suddenly, the boom was on. Boaters arrived, followed by new apartment complexes (Tahiti Marina Apartments, Marina Point Harbor, Villa Venetia, South Bay Apartments), shopping centers and restaurants. Pieces of Eight was the first restaurant to locate in the Marina. Then came the Warehouse, Cyrano's, Fiasco, Donkin's Inn, The Randy Tar, Lobster House, the Captain's Wharf and Don the Beachcomber. Fisherman's Wharf, with its Cape Cod Village shops, opened in 1969, joining Marina City West and Marina Shopping Center. Today, Marina del Rey, with nearly six thousand recreational boat slips and surrounding restaurants, shops, high-rise condominiums, apartments and hotels, is recognized as the world's largest small-craft harbor.

Clockwise from top: The Warehouse Restaurant, 1969.

The Warehouse's atmospheric South Seas approach over a koi-filled lagoon.

Logotype for Fiasco Restaurant.

Pieces of Eight, Marina del Rey's first restaurant.

The waterfront Marina del Rey Hotel, ca. 1970.

The lushly landscaped entry to Don the Beachcomber, a Polynesian restaurant-in-the-round famous for its Scorpion cocktail, ca. 1970.

fiasco
A SUPERLATIVE RESTAURANT
MARINA DEL REY, CALIFORNIA

DECORATIVE
ART
OF THE
TIMES

The Salvation Army band plays along Ocean Front Walk as chess players concentrate on their games, 1966.

Bottom right: First vehicles "christen" the last link of the Santa Monica Freeway on Opening Day, 1966, bringing surrounding communities that much closer to the Bay Area.

Below: Constructing the new Fourth Street on-ramp to the eastbound freeway, 1992.

Above: Fishermen greet the morning at the end of Santa Monica Pier, ca. 1966.

Top left: The new Venice Pier, at the foot of Washington Boulevard, was officially dedicated on February 27, 1965. Damage from corrosion led to the pier's closing in November 1986. It reopened in 1997.

Bottom left: Santa Monica Shores, twin seventeen-story structures covering five acres, is shown at lower center in this aerial view. The buildings were completed in 1966 as part of the Ocean Park Redevelopment Agency plan, offering 532 apartments, an Olympic twenty-five-meter pool and a nine-hole golf course.

The "Pink Lady" of
Malibu, ca. 1966. Artist
Lynne Westmore's sixty-
foot-tall painting of a
naked woman above
the tunnel on Malibu
Canyon Road was
deemed distracting to
drivers and sentenced
to quick elimination.
Here, workers armed
with spray-paint guns
and ropes start the climb
up the mountain wall.

Left: Groundbreaking for the $2.6 million County Administration Center in Malibu was held on May 27, 1968. The ceremony included (left to right) Judge John J. Merrick; Peter J. Pitchess, Sheriff, L.A. County; the Hon. Burton W. Chace; Father Godfrey McSweeney; Pierce Sherman; and pioneer realtor Lindsay Gillis.

The new Malibu Civic Center, above, with its dramatic colonnade, opened in the spring of 1970, housing the Malibu Justice Court, Branch Library and administrative and emergency housing offices. While proud Malibuites claimed, "Now we finally have a place to be from," the folks down the road trumpeted, "Santa Monica, where the action is!"

Saint Augustine-by-the-Sea Episcopal Church, the oldest church in Santa Monica still in its original location, on Fourth Street. The original redwood church, built in 1888, was destroyed by fire in 1966. The new structure was dedicated in 1969.

RESTAURANTS OF THE DAY

Clockwise from top left:
Tonga Lei, Malibu.

Jack's at the Beach, Ocean
Park Pier.

Uncle John's, Santa
Monica.

Santa Ynez Inn, Pacific
Palisades.

The Broken Drum ("You
can't beat it!"), Santa
Monica.

Clockwise from top left:
The Horn, Santa Monica.

Sinbad's, Santa Monica
Pier.

Bow & Arrow Restaurant
(William Tell Motel),
Santa Monica.

Cheerio, Santa Monica.

The Penguin, Santa
Monica.

Ted's Rancho, Malibu.

Alice's Restaurant,
Malibu Pier.

Top left: The southeast corner of Ocean Avenue and Wilshire Boulevard in April 1970. Construction of the Lawrence Welk Plaza (General Telephone Company building and Champagne Towers Apartments) was in its initial stages.

Top right: The finished complex dramatically changed the Santa Monica skyline.

With the opening of Temescal Canyon—from Sunset Boulevard to Pacific Coast Highway—to through traffic in the early 1970s, drivers received another bonus. Surrounding a long portion of the winding roadway, a scenic parkland was created, complete with trails and semi-enclosed picnic grounds.

Rose Avenue and Ocean Front Walk, 1973.

Through the morning haze, the Santa Monica skyline stands silhouetted against the eastern sky, 1973.

Beachfront houses hug Pacific Coast Highway just south of Topanga Canyon, 1973. Nearly eighty homes along a 1.25-mile stretch northward were razed by the state in 1974 to return the beach between Coastline Drive and Topanga Beach to its natural condition. Development on the palisade overlooking the area is Sunset Mesa.

TOPANGA BEACH, 1973

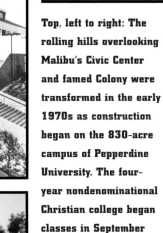

Top, left to right: The rolling hills overlooking Malibu's Civic Center and famed Colony were transformed in the early 1970s as construction began on the 830-acre campus of Pepperdine University. The four-year nondenominational Christian college began classes in September 1973.

Left: Serra Retreat, one of six Franciscan sanctuaries in the West, rises from Laudamus Hill in Malibu Canyon. The location was originally the site of a proposed Rindge mansion. In the 1930s, however, financial problems and the death of Mrs. Rindge halted construction—but not before she had invested more than five hundred thousand dollars in marble, tile and hand-carved mahogany. In 1941, for fifty thousand dollars, the Western Providence of the Franciscan Order bought the twenty-six-acre hilltop property, including the half-finished, neglected building. Two years later, after erecting a twenty-seven-room dormitory and renovating the mansion, the friars opened the sanctuary. The Malibu fire of 1970 destroyed all of Serra Retreat but the Memorial Wing. A new thirty-five-thousand-dollar facility, consisting of a small chapel, offices and sleeping accommodations for fifty-five, opened in January 1974.

Above and right: The northwest corner of Third Street and Wilshire Boulevard, long a gathering spot for residents and visitors attracted to the international atmosphere of its "shoppes and pubs," 1973. The nine-story black-glass Searise Building opened on the site in 1975.

The first section of the beach bike path was installed in 1974 (below, a portion south of Ocean Park Pier just prior to its being razed). The last leg was set in place in 1985, taking it through Santa Monica despite protests from Gold Coast home-owners. The bike path runs twenty-plus miles along the Bay from Temescal Canyon in Pacific Palisades south to Redondo Beach.

Bicycling along the beach in Santa Monica, 1996.

Top left: First Presbyterian Church at Second Street and Arizona Avenue, built in 1922, before its demolition in 1975, which made way for the Wilshire Palisades Building. The new First Presbyterian Church can be seen under construction at the right side of the photo. (The original First Presbyterian Church in Santa Monica was erected in 1887 on property at Third Street and Arizona donated by Senator John P. Jones, later the site of the Criterion Theater, now Mann's Criterion on the Third Street Promenade).

Bottom left: At the groundbreaking ceremony for the new First Presbyterian Church, California governor Ronald Reagan and his wife, Nancy, joined church officials and members, including the Rev. Ed Jones, interim pastor, and Dr. Marion Simms (both at far left of photo), November 1974.

The original J. Paul Getty Museum, which began as an extension to Getty's Malibu residence, first opened to the public in 1954. Consisting of eight galleries, it contained the art collection he started in the 1930s. The new museum, standing just below the old one, opened in January 1974. A reconstruction of a massive Roman seaside villa at Herculeneum (near Pompeii) that was destroyed in the eruption of Vesuvius in A.D. 79, it was designed to house three major collections—Western European Paintings, Greek and Roman Antiquities and French Decorative Arts—within thirty-eight galleries. The seventy-nine-thousand-square-foot, ten-acre structure incorporates colonnaded walkways, formal gardens, pools, fountains, mosaics, frescoes and plantings faithful to the original.

In 1994, it was announced that the museum would close in 1997 for a four-year renovation, reopening in the year 2001 as the Getty Villa, America's only museum devoted entirely to Greek and Roman art. With the exception of the antiquities, all of the museum's collections will be permanently held at the new Getty Center in Brentwood.

1875 / 1975

The year 1975 was a historic milestone for Santa Monica: the hundredth anniversary of the city's founding. It was a year filled with festivities, from the opening party hosted by the Centennial Committee, to the lavish Centennial Ball. In between, there were parades, concerts and numerous events to honor the descendants of the land-grant families and the individuals who played a part in shaping the growth of the city "where the mountains meet the sea."

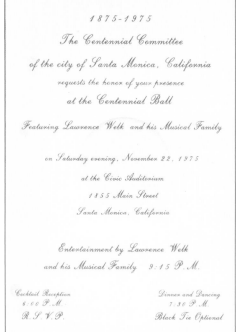

1875–1975

The Centennial Committee

of the city of Santa Monica, California

requests the honor of your presence

at the Centennial Ball

Featuring Lawrence Welk and his Musical Family

on Saturday evening, November 22, 1975

at the Civic Auditorium

1855 Main Street

Santa Monica, California

Entertainment by Lawrence Welk

and his Musical Family   9:15 P.M.

Cocktail Reception   *Dinner and Dancing*
6:00 P.M.   *7:30 P.M.*
R.S.V.P.   *Black Tie Optional*

Invitation to the Centennial Ball.

Verne Reynolds of the First Presbyterian Church places items from 1975 in a cornerstone of the new church building, to be opened in the year 2075. Among the sealed materials were coins from 1875, a 1975 Sears catalog, special Centennial editions of the *Santa Monica Outlook* newspaper, and a first edition of the book *Santa Monica Bay: The First 100 Years*.

Lawrence Welk, one of Santa Monica's famous "sons," entertained with his musical family at the Centennial Ball, 1975.

Joggers run along the surf line south of Santa Monica Pier during the late afternoon, mid-1970s.

Business Park, a $60 million development fronting Ocean Park Boulevard between Twenty-eighth and Thirty-first Streets, began taking shape during the late 1970s on the fifty-seven-acre site formerly occupied by Douglas Aircraft Company. The sprawling complex includes both commercial and industrial buildings, as well as Clover Park, the second largest recreational park in Santa Monica.

Patrick's Roadhouse in Santa Monica Canyon, opened in the mid-1970s, has become a favorite place to eat for beachgoers as well as celebrities. The onetime Red Car stop, hot dog stand and adjoining Entrada Motel has served the likes of Arnold Schwarzenegger, Ted Danson, Sylvester Stallone, Julia Roberts, numerous studio executives and President Bill Clinton.

Top right: The open spaces south of Malibu's new Civic Center, once planted with acres of commercially grown flowers, began to disappear in the late 1970s as new shops and offices were added to the busy center.

Ocean Park's Main Street experienced a renaissance during the 1970s, spurred by a contemporary spirit and an influx of new business. Adding to the existing creative climate were an array of distinctive antique and specialty shops, art galleries and uniquely themed restaurants.

In 1979, Twenty-second Street, from Arizona Avenue to Santa Monica Boulevard, was closed to through traffic and became part of Saint John's Hospital and Health Center's new forecourt.

One of Malibu's most publicized landslides occurred on April 14, 1979, in the Big Rock area when tons of earth and rock rumbled onto Pacific Coast Highway. Unstable conditions prompted the building of an immense "wall" of steel and wood girders to protect motorists and nearby homes.

Top left: Groundbreaking ceremonies for First Federal Square, a new twelve-story office complex, took place in July 1979. The prismatic-shaped Main Tower, set back from Wilshire Boulevard (between Fourth and Fifth Streets) by a progressive step-back of floors, slopes up from the landscaped ground-level plaza.

Top right: The Wilshire Palisades Building, an eleven-story office development overlooking Palisades Park, was the final phase of the Lawrence Welk Plaza at the foot of Wilshire Boulevard. The unique parallelogram shape of the terraced structure began rising soon after breaking ground in September 1979. (On one of the upper floor terraces, Lawrence Welk once had installed a putting green when back problems kept him from playing golf.)

Below: Zuma Beach in Malibu, once a muddy catch-basin for the swampy lowlands of Ramirez Canyon, is today one of Southern California's most popular oceanside playgrounds. Shown here is the entrance to Zuma Beach in 1979. A new entry with mission-style tiled archways was part of a $9.4 million improvement program unveiled in October 1996.

The Mayfair Music Hall, previously the Mayfair Theater and, originally, the Majestic Theater at 214 Santa Monica Boulevard, was built in 1911 by Charles Tegner and J. Euclid Miles (of the Miles Playhouse). The elaborate façade, shown here in 1979, was restored in 1973. Once called the oldest legitimate theater operating in Los Angeles, it has been closed since the 1994 Northridge earthquake.

Artist's rendering of
the proposed Broadway
entrance to Santa
Monica Place, 1979.

SANTA MONICA PLACE

Santa Monica Place, a dramatic, three-level shopping mall, opened in late 1980. The huge center consists of over 160 shops, services and restaurants, two major department stores, park-like courts and pedestrian walkways with fountains, pools and plantings of trees, shrubs and flowers. A decade later, the shopping-mall-by-the-sea underwent a $15 million renovation that included the addition of new skylights, a drip fountain in the center court, interior plantings of palm trees and numerous decorative touches inside and out.

Before and after: the Second Street entrance to Santa Monica Place during construction in early 1980 (top photo) and in 1991 (middle photo).

Bottom: Interior view of Santa Monica Place, 1991.

Above: A mural depicting the St. Monica High School nickname, Mariners, was donated by the class of 1983. It runs along the school's façade on Washington Avenue.

In 1984, Santa Monica initiated its Twilight Dance series on Santa Monica Pier. The Thursday evening summerlong series, running from July through early September, has featured a broad mix of musical styles—from country, surf and Zydeco to Latin, jazz, reggae, blues and Celtic rock.

Top right: The opening of the 1987 season attracted five thousand people to dance to the music of the Rhythm Kings. Other performers over the years have included the Beach Boys, the Blasters, Dick Dale and the Del-tones, Beausoleil, and Queen Ida and her Zydeco Band.

Right: Civic officials join Miss Santa Monica to signal the official opening of the Tourist Information Center in Palisades Park on July 2, 1962.

Thousands of spectators jam Ocean and California Avenues to await the arrival of the Olympic torch during the torch relay through Santa Monica on the morning of July 14, 1984. The torch was carried up the California Incline by O. J. Simpson.

In 1984, a newly designed Tourist Information Center opened in time to serve visitors attending the Olympic Games in Los Angeles.

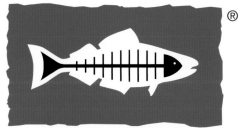

Heal the Bay

Founded in 1985, Heal the Bay is a nonprofit advocacy group of more than ten thousand members working to restore and enhance Southern California beaches and coastal waters for people and marine life through ongoing research, education, community action and policy programs.

Top left: Thousands of volunteers gather each year on Earth Day to clean up the coastal beaches.

Middle left: Part of the large Santa Monica contingent taking part in Hands Across America—a demonstration of compassion for America's homeless and hungry—along Ocean Avenue on May 25, 1986.

Bottom left: Guests gather in Palisades Park to await the unveiling of a monument honoring Arcadia Bandini de Baker at the core of the rose garden, October 1987. Along with Senator John P. Jones, Baker donated the parkland that overlooks Santa Monica Bay.

Opposite page: By the early 1980s, after nearly three-quarters of a century in Palisades Park, the base of the historic wooden pergola, set in soil, showed signs of deterioration and rot. During the late winter and spring of 1984, the entire structure was dismantled—slat by slat, timber by timber—and reassembled on a concrete base. Fencing along the length of the park was also replaced for Olympics sightseers.

Above: *Gestation 3*, an outdoor sculpture by California artist Baile Oakes, can be seen near the rose garden in Palisades Park.

Bottom right: On location at Marina del Rey's main channel, the cast and crew of *Baywatch* await filming. (Star David Hasselhoff stands at the front of the pontoon boat in red shorts and white shirt.) The series first aired in 1989, and has since become the world's most-watched television program—over one billion viewers tune in each week—and has introduced countless millions to the beauty of Santa Monica Bay, where exterior scenes are filmed. (*Pacific Blue*, an action series filmed mostly in Venice even though it is based on Santa Monica's bike patrol, premiered on cable TV in 1995.)

Above: *The Big Wave*, a forty-two-foot-tall steel loop, was installed over Wilshire Boulevard at the Franklin Street gateway to Santa Monica in June 1989. The work of artist Tony DeLap, *The Big Wave* was the first public art project approved by the city's Arts Commission when it was formed in 1982. Others followed, including the *Singing Beach Chairs* sculpture bench in Palisades Park, the *Santa Monica Timeline* mural at the Main Library, and *Gestation 3* in Palisades Park.

Above: Performance in Palisades Park: The history of Santa Monica is depicted in pantomime by young actors on a late afternoon in October 1986.

Left: Jonathan Borofsky's *Ballerina Clown*, perched on a tiny pedestal above the northwest corner of Main Street and Rose Avenue in Venice, has become a local landmark.

The Museum of Flying at Santa Monica Airport, on virtually the same spot where Douglas Airport was founded in 1922, opened in 1989 within a contemporary three-story structure of steel and glass, which houses extensive exhibits of aviation past and present. Some aircraft are dramatically suspended from the ceiling, while others are displayed along the museum's flight-line tarmac adjacent to a hangar door that is open to the airport's busy runway outside.

Clockwise from top left:

The Improv.

Greyhound Bus Station.

Mermaid Cafe.

Tex's Ski Shop.

The Oar House.

Biff's Coffee Shop.

At My Place.

Clockwise from top:

Zucky's.

Madame Wong's West (formerly Fox & Hounds Restaurant).

Fireside Market.

Pioneer Boulangerie.

Crown & Archer.

Top: Coral trees along the parkway (the old Red Car right-of-way) dividing Santa Monica's San Vicente Boulevard. A native of South Africa, the coral tree (*Erythrina caffra*) is particularly spectacular when in bloom. In late winter, after most of the leaves have dropped, the spreading branches become a mass of brilliant red-orange flowers. The trees may also be seen along the parkway dividing Olympic Boulevard. The first coral tree in Southern California is said to have been planted on Vaquero Hill in Malibu.

Above and right: Loews Santa Monica Beach Hotel, with its soaring glass-domed lobby, opened in 1989 on virtually the same site as the city's early grand hotel, the Arcadia. Loews has hosted the American Film Market since 1991.

In the planning stages for three years, a new concept for the Third Street Mall began to take shape in the late 1980s and culminated with the opening of the Third Street Promenade in 1989. Stretching from Broadway north to Wilshire Boulevard, the Promenade quickly captured the attention of a public that was drawn to its lively mix of theaters, shops, restaurants, sidewalk concerts and outdoor festivals.

The Frank Gehry–designed Edgemar complex (site of the 1908 Edgemar Dairy) on Main Street, Santa Monica's original "in" shopping area, is a minimall with an innovative twist. Set within its abstract forms are numerous high-profile establishments such as Röckenwagner restaurant.

Aerial view of Santa Monica Bay
at twilight, looking north from
midtown Santa Monica toward
Malibu, ca. 1991.

Top left: Malibu's old sheriff's station on Pacific Coast Highway.

Middle left: Malibu High School, overlooking Zuma Beach, opened in the fall of 1992. (Students previously had to travel to Santa Monica High for classes.) The school graduated its first class of seniors in May 1996.

Below: A shark, the Malibu High emblem, adorns one of the entry walls.

Bottom left: The "back side" of Point Dume in Malibu, a popular location for television and motion picture filming.

Bottom right: The lush tropical oasis that is the Colony Plaza shopping center in Malibu.

Pacific Coast Highway snakes past Malibu Pier in this 1991 aerial view. At upper right, Malibu Creek empties into the Malibu Lagoon, a wildlife preserve. Between the lagoon and the pier are the historic Adamson House and Surfrider State Beach. (As early as the 1940s, the cove at Surfrider, formerly known as Keller's Shelter, was known as a "paradise for surf-riders," who boasted that it offered the finest surfboard riding in the world, surpassing even Waikiki Beach.) Malibu gained cityhood—and its independence—on March 28, 1991.

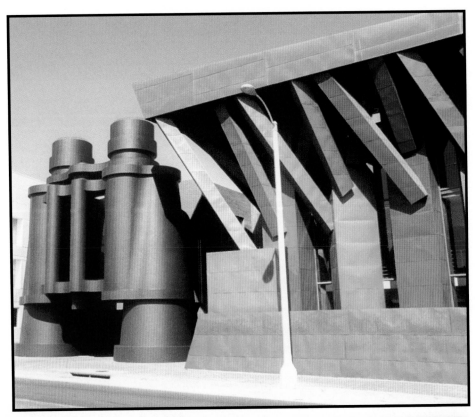

Right: A three-story pair of binoculars forms the entry to the building designed by Frank Gehry for Chiat Day Advertising Agency in Venice. Completed in 1991, visitors must reach the structure's underground garage by driving between the upright lenses. The eyepieces serve as skylights illuminating the interior of the binoculars, which open onto a large conference room.

Above: Pulitzer Prize–winning cartoonist Paul Conrad's twenty-six-foot-tall atomic cloud sculpture, *Chain Reaction*, made of giant chain links as a symbol of world peace, was installed on the lawn of the Santa Monica Civic Auditorium in 1991.

Right: In the years that followed Muscle Beach's move from Santa Monica to Venice, the weight-lifting facility was known simply as "the pit." In 1990, construction began on a new, and larger, Muscle Beach stage, bleachers and sculpture in the form of a massive set of barbells. The $516,000 renovation was dedicated on September 10, 1991.

The Water Garden office complex in Santa Monica consists of four six-story buildings, fountains, waterfalls, a lake, bridges, gazebos and parklands within its seventeen-acre site. Phase I of the 1.2-million-square-foot project opened in early 1992.

Shutters on the Beach, a 198-room luxury hotel that opens directly onto the sands of Santa Monica, was completed in June 1993. The hotel's architecture evokes memories of beach resorts and cottages from another, more gentle, era.

Mini amusement area, primarily a summertime attraction for children adjacent to the carousel on Santa Monica Pier, 1993.

On the afternoon of
November 3, 1993, it
appeared that storm
clouds were approaching
on the horizon. But the
news was not about rain.
A fire was raging in
Malibu, whipped by
high winds that were
sweeping across the
mountains and canyons
from Coral Canyon to
Topanga toward the
shore. Five thousand
firefighters battled the
blaze for days; when
the smoke had finally
cleared, over thirty-five
thousand acres and two
hundred homes had been
scorched. It was not the
first of the area's fires,
but it was among the
most destructive.
Contrary to one headline
that appeared in the
papers, however,
paradise was not lost.

Signs, made by grateful homeowners to thank firefighters, appeared throughout Malibu after the fire.

THANK YOU GOD BLESS YOU

The Miramar Hotel celebrated its hundredth anniversary in 1989 with a $33 million renovation that lasted into the 1990s. There were extensive changes throughout—not only within but to the exterior as well. The bungalows that opened onto the pool area, built in 1938, were leveled and replaced with luxury one- and two-story structures. A new pool was installed, along with new landscaping that included waterfalls, ponds, walkways and decking. An impressive new Wilshire Boulevard main entrance was created, replacing the former entry on Ocean Avenue. Here, the decorative wrought-iron gate at the new Wilshire entrance to the Miramar Sheraton Hotel.

One of the first sights for visitors on entering the grounds to the Miramar is the historic Moreton Bay fig tree (*Ficus macrophylla*), planted in 1879 by Senator John P. Jones. It is the sole reminder of his elegant estate, Miramar, which once covered the square-block area bounded by Ocean and California Avenues, Wilshire Boulevard and Second Street.

President Bill Clinton (left) sets the pace as he jogs along the Santa Monica beachfront, 1995. The president has been a frequent visitor to Santa Monica and the Miramar during his administration.

Surrounded by early morning fog, Ocean Avenue is barricaded and clogged with police and media vehicles during one of President Clinton's stays at the Miramar.

Marina del Rey skyline
from the cylindrical
towers of the Marina
City Club to the Ritz-
Carlton Hotel, 1994.

Mother's Beach, Marina
del Rey, 1994.

Below left: The spacious pool area at the Ritz-Carlton Hotel in Marina del Rey. The 306-room luxury hotel opened in late 1990.

Below right: A holiday tradition at Marina del Rey since 1963, the annual Christmas Boat Parade features festively decorated power yachts and sailboats plus fireworks, live bands and singing groups. The floating parade makes its way along the Marina's main channel.

JANUARY 17, 1994

I t happened without warning in the predawn hour of 4:31 A.M. Walls shook, windows shattered, chimneys fell, buildings crumbled. A deadly magnitude 6.6 earthquake—the strongest in modern Los Angeles history—rumbled for ten seemingly endless seconds, triggered by a fault that squeezed the northern San Fernando Valley between two mountain ranges like a vise. Although many miles away from the epicenter in Northridge, California, the Bay Area was not left untouched. Santa Monica, in particular, felt the force of the quake with damage reported in various sections of the city. Much of the area was left without visible scarring, but no one present that morning will ever forget those few terrifying seconds—or the days that followed.

A NEW SPIRIT

In moments of tragedy, it is said, people pull together. That was certainly evident throughout the post-quake days and weeks of 1994. It was a time for renewal, and for offering a helping hand. Signs of recovery were everywhere, from storefronts to buildings girdled with scaffolding. The cleanup brought a new shine to the city, and with it, a new spirit.

WE'RE
BOUNCING
BACK.

Crowds line up for
tickets to attend
performances of Cirque
du Soleil's innovative
big-top show during
its 1994 visit to
Santa Monica.

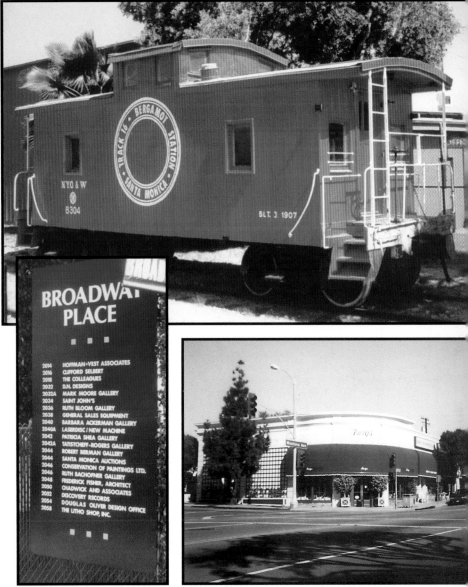

Top and above left: Artists have long been drawn to the beach area, but during the 1990s Santa Monica became home to some of the West's finest art galleries. Many are concentrated along Colorado Avenue, Broadway, Main Street and, in the newest arts complex, Bergamot Station (named for a Red Car trolley station that occupied the site until the 1950s).

Above right: Fashionable Montana Avenue, 1994. Once best known for its service stations, laundromats and neighborhood stores, Montana is now famous for its boutiques, restaurants and sidewalk cafes.

Above: The new
Venice–Abbot Kinney
Memorial Branch Library
opened in August 1995
with a performance
by the Venice Arts
Mecca Youth Orchestra.
It was designed by
postmodernist architect
Michael Graves, working
as consultant with Ernest
P. Howard Associates.

Right: Palisades High
School, home of the
Dolphins, 1996. The
campus opened in
September 1961.

Left: Entrance to the Mediterranean-style clubhouse of the Bel Air Bay Club, 1996. The clubhouse and grounds, on seven acres rising ninety feet above the club's private facilities on the beach below, were designed by architect Elmer Grey and landscape architect Mark Daniels, and dedicated in 1930. The Bel Air Bay Club was founded by developer Alphonso E. Bell, who served as president from 1927 to 1945.

Below: Entrance to Santa Monica Hospital, 1994. In 1995, the hospital joined with UCLA to form the Santa Monica–UCLA Medical Center.

Top right: Thousands of onlookers turn out for the annual Festival of the Chariots along Ocean Front Walk in Venice. Floats four stories tall are pulled along the boardwalk from Santa Monica Pier to the Venice Pavilion.

Bottom right: Volleyball courts at Will Rogers State Beach across from Santa Monica Canyon, 1996. It is believed that volleyball courts were first introduced in 1924 at the Beach Club, a few steps south of State Beach. Around 1950, in the same location, the first men's doubles tournaments took place. Since then, volleyball has become one of America's fastest-growing sports. Both indoor and beach volleyball were events at the 1996 Summer Olympics.

Below: The Beach Club logo, 1928.

Left and above: Memories of the 1984 Olympics were revived as the torch run for the 1996 Olympics passed through Santa Monica on its way to Atlanta, Georgia. Here, on Wilshire Boulevard, traffic is at a standstill as crowds gather to cheer on the young torchbearer and his escorts.

Bottom left: Motorcycle corps, drill teams, bicycle and mounted patrols, and vintage automobiles transporting celebrities and city officials helped honor the hundredth anniversary of the Santa Monica Police Department with a parade down Ocean Avenue, 1996.

Pacific Park, a $12 million, open-air family amusement park on Santa Monica Pier, opened to the public on May 25, 1996. The West Coast's only amusement park located on an oceanfront pier features eleven rides for children and adults, such as the Santa Monica West Coaster roller coaster, the giant Pacific Wheel ferris wheel (towering nine stories high), Sea Dragon, Rock and Roll, and a bumper-car ride called Sig Alert. Games, food, merchandise, and entertainment are also attractions. Pacific Park, along with the pier's historic carousel, UCLA's Ocean Discovery Center, and the Ash Grove nightclub, marks a return to the golden age of Southern California's pleasure piers.

IN HONOR
OF
JOHN P. JONES
FOUNDER OF
SANTA MONICA AND
FOR THIRTY YEARS A
SENATOR OF
THE UNITED STATES
PIONEER OF THE WEST
STATESMAN PHILOSOPHER
FRIEND

ON THE SPOT
HE LOVED SO WELL
THIS MEMORIAL HAS BEEN
ERECTED IN RECOGNITION
OF HIS SERVICES TO
THE CITY OF SANTA MONICA
AND TO
THE NATION

This circular stone bench, a memorial to Senator John P. Jones, Santa Monica's founder, is located in Palisades Park directly across the street from the site of his estate, Miramar. The inscription reads: "In the evening of his life, John P. Jones used to come each day to watch the sun set over the ocean."

Epilogue

Today, the waters of the Bay are as placid, the curve of the shoreline as lovely, and the rise of its bluffs as imposing as when Juan Cabrillo and his men cast anchor centuries ago. From the "Bay of Smokes" to a verdant pasture, from a struggling village to an internationally famous playground, from a handful of isolated towns to a sprawling cosmopolitan center, the Bay Area is a thriving panorama so vast that not even the Bakers, Joneses, Rindges, Kinneys and other giants of the formative years could imagine its equal, even in their finest hour. Indeed, it is a panorama that would amaze anyone who has not been around to witness the progress that has taken place.

In the twenty-plus years since the Santa Monica Centennial and the publication of *Santa Monica Bay: The First 100 Years*, the Bay Area has undergone many stunning changes. The last several years alone have seen the creation of the Third Street Promenade and the Pacific Park "fun zone." Luxury hotels have risen, along with centers for the arts. Trendsetting restaurants have opened—Michael's, Chinois on Main, I Cugini, Schatzi on Main—and entertainment giants, such as Metro-Goldwyn-Mayer, Sony Music, Columbia Records, Epic Records, MTV Networks and the National Academy of Recording Arts and Sciences have made the coastal area their home. And Malibu has become a city.

There is more in the planning stages: renovation of the Venice boardwalk and pavilion; a new Santa Monica breakwater (to replace the breakwater that was dashed during the 1983 winter storms) and boat harbor, along with a new Civic Center; a new look for Main Street; a marine refuge along Malibu's twenty-seven-mile coastline; new beachfront hotels; and Santa Monica Studios, a state-of-the-art entertainment complex.

Historically rich Santa Monica Bay, paradise by the sea, looks forward to an even more abundant tomorrow.

Acknowledgments

Special thanks to the following contributors for their generous assistance and cooperation in providing historical data and illustrative materials:

Michael Allan *(Will Rogers State Historical Park)*
Richard Ameny *(Brentwood Country Club)*
Robert L. Armacost
Dorothy Jones Boden
Ralph Cantos
Tom Carroll
Richard Michael Cibener
Zola Clearwater
Robert E. Cody *(Security Pacific Bank)*
Lura Dymond *(Westways magazine)*
Bill Ferrell *(General Telephone Company)*
Russell Gates *(Bel Air Bay Club)*
Sue Gessler *(General Telephone Company)*
Don Girard *(Santa Monica College)*
Phil Gray *(Santa Monica Hospital)*
Jack Hageny
Jane and Joe Hecht
Phil Hill
Koli Communications
Jennie Kraft
Larry Lee
James Lennon
Los Angeles County Fire Department, Lifeguard Division
Ernie Marquez
Marty Morehart *(Malibu Feed Bin)*
Cynthia Murphy *(Santa Monica Library)*
Dolorez Nariman *(Title Insurance & Trust Company)*

Nancy O'Neill *(Santa Monica Library)*
Angie Otterstrom
Charles Phoenix
Audrey Bishop Plant
Toni Pogue *(Heal the Bay)*
Carol Rang *(Pelico and Associates)*
Frances Rehwald *(W. I. Simonson, Inc.)*
Skip Rimer *(Santa Monica Outlook)*
Liz Roberson
Frances Roberts *(Saint John's Hospital)*
Daniel J. Ryan *(Museum of Flying)*
George and Grace Shehady
Sally Shishmanian
Larry Smith *(California Federal Savings & Loan Association)*
Maris Somerville *(Somerville Associates)*
Jeff Stanton
Harry and Madeline Strangman
Ken Strickfaden
John Sweeney *(Santa Monica Outlook)*
Carl Tegner
Martha Townsend *(Santa Monica Library)*
Ed Tynan *(Boulevard Camera)*
Neil Van Scoten
Clyde Walker
Sue Waller *(J. Paul Getty Museum)*
Bill Youngs *(Pepperdine University)*

Photo Credits

Index